Hebrew Bible

Book of

Numbers

Five books of Moses

SimchatChaim.com

There is no known book without mistakes. Therefore, I ask in every language of application if anyone has any questions, comments, clarifications, corrections, please send to: simchatchaim@yahoo.com

All material used in this section may not be used for commercial purposes, but only for study and teaching.

To get this book or books and information Email me at:

simchatchaim@yahoo.com

מהדורה שניה תשפ"ד
Second edition 2024

The contents of the book

Page   Chapter

Introduction to the

Jewish Bible

First you need to know that the Bible was originally written in the holy language, which today is called Hebrew.

The Tanach itself went through a series of translations from language to language until today's English language.

As a whole, the Tanakh was translated from the holy language into Greek, and from Greek into Latin, and from there into the ancient Agalic, and then into the more modern English.

The problem is when translating from language to language the original meaning is lost.

In the translation of languages there is no realistic possibility to make a completely accurate translation, since in every language there are several translation options for most words, and each word has a different connotation, and also differs to a certain extent from the exact connotation of the original word in the source language.

For example, it is possible to translate the word - שמים. **sky** into English for Sky and Heaven. Two suitable options that each have a different meaning from the other, and also slightly different from the full connotation of the word **sky שמים**. For this reason, along with the attempt to bridge the cultural difference, every translation is actually also an interpretation. In many cases, the translators took the approach of **extensive translation**, in which the translation adds details and interpretations beyond the original text, changes the content, and describes what is happening in a way that is more suitable to the cultural concepts accepted for the period and region. In the common translations these changes are found - to a certain degree of change - in tens of percent of the verses. The general public in these periods knew the Bible only from the translations, and therefore in different regions they actually knew different versions of the same texts, according to the local halachic belief.

The most classic example of this is this:
In the book of Exodus chapter 34 verse 29 it is explained that - KARAN [קרן] the skin of Moses face.

The word KARAN [קרן] has at least two meanings:
A. Radiant.
B. A horn, like that of a bull.
There are other meanings to this word that do not belong to this introduction.

An incorrect translation of the Book of Exodus by Jerome [the Vulgate] into Latin led to an error in the interpretation of the phrase - The horn of the skin of his face. [Exodus 34:29]. And because of this, in

Renaissance sculptures, Moshe's forehead was added **Horns**.

And this is the verse in its entirety according to our translation [compare it to your Bible] - So Moses came down from Mount Sinai. And as Moses came down from the mountain bearing the two tablets of the Pact, Moses was not aware that the skin of his face was **radiant**, since he had spoken with God.

It is known that Hebrew has a vowel for every word. And there can be a word that has a different vowel from the same word. For example, the word with four letters - מ.ד.ב.ר

מְדַבֵּר - speaker.

מִדְבָּר - desert.

מְדַבֵּר - A speaking man.

מִדָּבָר - out of nothing.

מְדֻבָּר - thing that is being discussed.

There are **only** five vowels with the same word, and really this word has 25 vowel types!!!! which can change the entire meaning of the verse and the translation.

The first translations of the Bible were created by Jews at the beginning of the first millennium AD. During this period, most Jews gradually stopped using the Hebrew language, especially biblical Hebrew. A translated Bible became a basic necessity for the reading of the Torah in the synagogues, which was performed by two people - one who read the verse is in the original language, and an interpreter repeats his words in the spoken language.

The first translations of the Bible were created by Jews at the beginning of the first millennium AD. During this period, most Jews gradually stopped using the Hebrew language, especially biblical Hebrew. A translated Bible became a basic necessity for the reading of the Torah in the synagogues, which was performed by two people - one who read the verse is in the original language, and an interpreter repeats his words in the spoken language.

The Bible translations can be divided into two main types - Jewish translations and Christian translations. There are a number of differences between the two, the most prominent of which is the inclusion of the New Testament in Christian translations as opposed to its absence in Jewish translations. The Jewish translations were made mainly from the original Hebrew text, and most of the early Jewish translations were made only into separate parts of the Bible, with the intention that they will be used as a commentary on the Bible. In contrast, the Christian translations are mostly intended for independent use, and most of them are based on the Greek translation translated into Latin - the Latin Vulgate.

The truth is that the Holy Scriptures should not be translated into any language. But because of an act explained in the Talmud there was no choice and the Jews translated it.

And the story is:
And this was due to the incident of King Ptolemy, as it is taught in a Baraita: There was an incident involving King Ptolemy of Egypt, who assembled seventy-two Elders from the Sages of Israel, and put them into seventy-two separate rooms, and did not reveal to them for what purpose he assembled them, so that they would not coordinate their responses. He entered and approached each and every one, and said to each of them: Write for me a translation of the Torah of Moses your teacher. The Holy One, Blessed be He, placed wisdom in the heart of each and every one, and they all agreed to one common understanding. Not only did they all translate the text correctly, they all introduced the same changes into the translated text.

And the Talmud [Megillah 9a] continues to say that all 72 sages did not translate it exactly, but changed several verses, for example:

And they wrote for him: God created in the beginning [**Bereshit**], reversing the order of the words in the first phrase in the Torah that could be misinterpreted as: **Bereshit created God** [Genesis 1:1]. Instead of: Come, let us go down, and there confound their language [Genesis 11:7], which indicates multiple authorities, they wrote in the singular: Come, let me go down, and there confound their language. In addition, they replaced the verse: "And Sarah laughed within herself [**bekirba**] [Genesis 18:12], with: And Sarah laughed among her relatives [**bikroveha**].

They made this change to distinguish between Sarah's laughter, which God criticized, and Abraham's laughter, to which no reaction is recorded. Based on the change, Sarah's laughter was offensive because she voiced it to others….

The church father Hieronymus [about 325-420], who knew Hebrew in addition to Latin and Greek, and specialized in theology, created an improved homogenous translation from all the Latin translations. In his work, which was done between the years 390-405, he was greatly assisted by the Jews he knew. The translation of the first books he dealt with [first prophets, Samuel and kings] was done closely to the Hebrew text, but the last books [Joshua, Judges, Ruth and Esther] were translated by him in a freer manner. In any case, Hieronymus relied on the Hebrew version, because he noticed the deviations that the Greek translations have from the Hebrew original.

The Vulgate was recognized by the Church in 1546 as the authoritative text of the Holy Scriptures. It includes, apart from the books of the Bible and the New Testament, also the translation of the external books. The name **Vulgate** [=Common] can be translated by Roger Bacon, and when the internal division into chapters was made in the Vulgate.

The English translation - a translation of parts of the Bible into English was made starting from the 7th century. A complete translation of the Bible into English, made under the direction of John Wycliffe, from the Latin version of the Vulgate, was published in about 1380. The church condemned this translation, because it saw the interpretation that accompanied it as heretical. Further English translations were also rejected by the church and the king.

In 1530 William Tyndale translated only the Pentateuch from the Greek in the Kaspela edition into English, and 5 years later Miles Coverdale published the entire Bible in English. James I, King of England initiated the creation of an official translation of the Bible and the New Testament into English. His initiative came against the background of the bitter struggle between Protestants and Catholics in England and Scotland. King James proposed to write a new English translation that would be acceptable to Protestants and Catholics alike. This translation, made from Hebrew and Greek, was published in 1611, and is called the "King James Version, KJV". This translation is still considered the authorized translation of the English Bible [Authorized Version]; Researchers from the universities of London, Oxford and Cambridge worked on it. They also used a Jewish commentary for the translation. In this edition, King James demanded to cleanse the kings of any evil that could cling to them, in order to purify the institution of the monarchy. In the translation, an effort was made to maintain the structure of the Hebrew text, and to convert as much as possible a Hebrew word into an English word. However, a Hebrew word may be translated into different words in English in different contexts, this is to keep the language fluid. The attempt to literally translate Hebrew idioms created new expressions in English, which gradually became part of the English language and culture.

The book of Numbers

Sefer [the book] **Be'Midbar** is the fourth book among the five pentacles of the Torah.

According to the testimony of Hieronymus, the book was called in his time: **Vidaber** and this name is also found in the medieval language of Avraham Ibn Ezra, in the sage tradition it is found under the name **Five Commandments**, and this is because it contains two commanders of the Israelites as well as another separate commander for the tribe of Levi This is also where the foreign names Ἀριθμοί in the Septuagint translation and Numeri in the Vulgate [meaning - **numbers**", as well as in English - Book of Numbers] came from. **Sefer Be'madbar** deals with the wandering of the Israelites in the desert, a period of about 40 years, between the departure from Egypt and the entry into the Land of Israel; And actually, focuses only on the beginning and end of this period.

Chapters 1-10
With the books of Exodus and Leviticus, the long process of the exodus from Egypt, receiving the Torah and building the tabernacle ends.

The people are ready to go on their wanderings.

The Book of the Desert begins by describing the preparations for the journey in four parts: the preparation of the people for the journey, the work of the Levites, special laws and the departure for the journey.

The Camp of Israel [Chapter 1 - Chapter 2]: The book begins with God's command to count the people of Israel at the beginning of the journey in the desert. After the census, the order of the camp is described in the breaks between journeys: in the center of the tabernacle, around it the priests and Levites, and around them the rest of the people of Israel camped in four flags on the four sides of the camp - three tribes in each flag.

The Levites [Chapter 3 - Chapter 4]: After the census of the Levites, the exchange of the firstborn with the Levites is described [the firstborn were originally supposed to be the servants of the tabernacle], and then a description of the work of the Levites during the journey: the sons of Kohath carry the vessels of the tabernacle, the sons of Gershon the cloth vessels of the tabernacle - And above it, and the sons of Marri, the planks of the tabernacle and everything related to them.

Special Laws [Chapter 5 - Chapter 9, Verse 14]: Law of a guilt sacrifice, law of a perverted woman, law of the monk, blessing of the priests [said to this day in the synagogues by the priests], sacrifices of the heads of the tribes, purity of the Levites and second Passover.

The departure for the journey in the desert [chapter 9, verse 15 - chapter 10]: The cloud determines the path of the Israelites - when they will travel and when they will camp, as well as the sounding of the trumpets -

in times of peace and war, and the departure itself when the ark is at the head of the camp.

This part ends with the poem - **And it was in the journey of the ark**, by Moshe, which is surrounded by the letters of the inverted NUN before and after it - for this several explanations have been proposed in the Talmud and commentaries.

Chapters 11-19

In these chapters many events are described that happened during the journey in the desert. The main events are the sins of the Israelites in the desert such as the sin of the lustful ones in the burning, the sin of the lustful in the graves of lust, the sin of the spies and Korach his committee.

The People's Grievances [Chapter 11]: The chapter begins with a description of God's anger over the people's complaint [the sin of the covetous] at Tabara, and continues with the people's complaints regarding the conditions of the journey and their longing for Egypt [the sin of the covetous]. Following this complaint, Moses despairs of the people, and God adds to him 70 Elders as help in leadership.

Miriam's leprosy [chapter 12]: Miriam gossips about Moshe together with Aaron ["Because a Kushite woman took..."] As a result, Miriam is afflicted with leprosy.

The sin of the spies [chapter 13 - chapter 14]: Moses sends 12 representatives to spy on the land. The spies pass through its southern parts and take its fruits. Upon their return, a debate develops as to whether the land can be conquered, with only Caleb ben Yefuna and Yehoshua ben Nun trying to convince the people to immigrate anyway. Following the hesitation, it was decreed that a generation of Egyptians would mostly perish in the desert, and only then would entry into the land be allowed. As a result, some try to make their way to the land, but their attempt fails [the sin of the immigrants] - the people turn to continue their journeys in the desert.

Various Laws [Chapter 15]: Offerings offered with the sacrifice: semolina, oil and wine. Sacrifices for the sins of a public or its representatives.

The controversy of Korah and his committee [chapter 16 - chapter 18, verse 7]: Korah and his committee disputed the leadership of Moshe and Aaron. As a test, Korah and his committee will burn incense, as well as Aharon. Fire consumed Korah's censers and all his men were swallowed up in the earth. In another test, Aaron's staff blossomed and testified that only Aaron and his sons [tribe of Levi] would be used in the Tabernacle.

Various laws [chapter 18, verse 8 - chapter 19]: the part of the priests in sacrifices and grain, under receiving an estate in the land, and the laws of a red cow.

Chapters 20-25

This part deals with events that happened on the border of the Land of Israel but are not directly related to entering the Land.

Disputed water [chapter 20, verses 1-13]: After the death of Miriam, the people quarreled with Moses because of a lack of water. God commands Moses to speak to the rock to bring out water, and Moses strikes the rock until water comes out of it. This case is mentioned later - As a reason for the punishment of Moshe and Aharon, following which they will not enter the land.

The death of Aaron the priest [chapter 20, verses 14-21]: the king of Edom prevents Israel from passing through his country who surround his country instead of fighting it. During the journey, Aharon died and was buried in Mount Hare.

The copper snake [chapter 21, verses 4-9]: Moses prepares a copper snake, according to God's instructions, to stop the killing of the people of Israel following a plague of snakes.

War of Sihon [chapter 21, verses 10-35]: The king of Arad fought Israel, and following another refusal, Sihon, the king of the Amorites [Bihetz], followed by Og, king of Bashan [Badrei].

Parashat Balaam [chapter 22 - chapter 24]: Balak, king of Moab [also a kingdom beyond the Jordan] brings Balaam, a sorcerer and prophet, to curse the Israelites. Balaam tries his strength, but blessings come out of his mouth instead of curses.

Act of Zimri [chapter 25] After Balaam leaves, the statesmen send their daughters to seduce Israel into prostitution. As a result, a plague breaks out among the people. Phinehas, the grandson of Aaron the priest, kills Zimri ben Salua. As a result, he is guaranteed that his descendants will serve as priests.

Chapters 26-36

In these chapters the preparations for the occupation of the land are detailed.

The end of the journey [chapter 26]: The Israelites

reach the plains of Moab and there another census of the people of Israel is made, including the tribe of Levi.

Daughters of Zelphad [chapter 27, verses 1-11]: The daughters of Zelphad turn to Moses with the question of whether they will be able to inherit the land, even though their father died without male offspring. Traces of their appeal God commanded the laws of inheritance, according to which daughters inherit their father when he has no male sons to inherit him.

The appointment of Joshua [chapter 27, verses 15-23]: Moses appoints Joshua ben Nun as his replacement.

Various laws [chapter 28 - chapter 4]: the sacrifices of the Tamim, the Moedim, and the laws of breaking vows.

War of Midin [chapter 31]: The Israelites take revenge on Midin for having wronged them in prostitution. The war ended in the defeat of Midin

Numbers

Bamidbar

Chapter 1

1. AND THE LORD spoke unto Moses in the wilderness of Sinai, in the tent of meeting, on the first day of the second month, in the second year after they were come out of the land of Egypt, saying:

2. Take ye the sum of all the congregation of the children of Israel, by their families, by their fathers' houses, according to the number of names, every male, by their polls;

3. From twenty years old and upward, all that are able to go forth to war in Israel: ye shall number them by their hosts, even thou and Aaron.

4. And with you there shall be a man of every tribe, every one head of his fathers' house.

5. And these are the names of the men that shall stand with you: of Reuben, Elizur the son of Shedeur.

6. Of Simeon, Shelumiel the son of Zurishaddai.

7. Of Judah, Nahshon the son of Amminadab.

8. Of Issachar, Nethanel the son of Zuar.

9. Of Zebulun, Eliab the son of Helon.

10. Of the children of Joseph: of Ephraim, Elishama the son of Ammihud; of Manasseh, Gamaliel the son of Pedahzur.

11. Of Benjamin, Abidan the son of Gideoni.

12. Of Dan, Ahiezer the son of Ammishaddai.

13. Of Asher, Pagiel the son of Ochran.

14. Of Gad, Eliasaph the son of Deuel.

15. Of Naphtali, Ahira the son of Enan.

16. These were the elect of the congregation, the princes of the tribes of their fathers; they were the heads of the thousands of Israel.

17. And Moses and Aaron took these men that are pointed out by name.

18. And they assembled all the congregation together on the first day of the second month, and they declared their pedigrees after their families, by their fathers' houses, according to the number of names, from twenty years old and upward, by their polls.

19. As the LORD commanded Moses, so did he number them in the wilderness of Sinai.

20. And the children of Reuben, Israel's first-born, their generations, by their families, by their fathers' houses, according to the number of names, by their polls, every male from twenty years old and upward, all that were able to go forth to war;

21. Those that were numbered of them, of the tribe of Reuben, were forty and six thousand and five hundred.

22. Of the children of Simeon, their generations, by their families, by their fathers' houses, those that were numbered thereof, according to the number of names, by their polls, every male from twenty years old and upward, all that were able to go forth to war;

23. Those that were numbered of them, of the tribe of Simeon, were fifty and nine thousand and three hundred.

24. Of the children of Gad, their generations, by their families, by their fathers' houses, according to the number of names, from twenty years old and upward, all that were able to go forth to war;

25. Those that were numbered of them, of the tribe of Gad, were forty and five thousand six hundred and fifty.

26. Of the children of Judah, their generations, by their families, by their fathers' houses, according to the number of names, from twenty years old and upward, all that were able to go forth to war;

27. Those that were numbered of them, of the tribe of Judah, were threescore and fourteen thousand and six hundred.

28. Of the children of Issachar, their generations, by their families, by their fathers' houses, according to the number of names, from twenty years old and upward, all that were able to go forth to war;

29. Those that were numbered of them, of the tribe of Issachar, were fifty and four thousand and four hundred.

30. Of the children of Zebulun, their generations, by their families, by their fathers' houses, according to the number of names, from twenty years old and upward, all that were able to go forth to war;

31. Those that were numbered of them, of the tribe of Zebulun, were fifty and seven thousand and four hundred.

32. Of the children of Joseph, namely, of the children of Ephraim, their generations, by their families, by their fathers' houses, according to the number of names, from twenty years old and upward, all that were able to go forth to war;

33. Those that were numbered of them, of the tribe of Ephraim, were forty thousand and five hundred.

34. Of the children of Manasseh, their generations, by their families, by their fathers' houses, according to the number of names, from twenty years old and upward, all that were able to go forth to war;

35. Those that were numbered of them, of the tribe of Manasseh, were thirty and two thousand and two hundred.

36. Of the children of Benjamin, their generations, by their families, by their fathers' houses, according to the number of names, from twenty years old and upward, all that were able to go forth to war;

37. Those that were numbered of them, of the tribe of Benjamin, were thirty and five thousand and four hundred.

38. Of the children of Dan, their generations, by their families, by their fathers' houses, according to the number of names, from twenty years old and upward, all that were able to go forth to war;

39. Those that were numbered of them, of the tribe of

Dan, were threescore and two thousand and seven hundred.

40. Of the children of Asher, their generations, by their families, by their fathers' houses, according to the number of names, from twenty years old and upward, all that were able to go forth to war;

41. Those that were numbered of them, of the tribe of Asher, were forty and one thousand and five hundred.

42. Of the children of Naphtali, their generations, by their families, by their fathers' houses, according to the number of names, from twenty years old and upward, all that were able to go forth to war;

43. Those that were numbered of them, of the tribe of Naphtali, were fifty and three thousand and four hundred.

44. These are those that were numbered, which Moses and Aaron numbered, and the princes of Israel, being twelve men; they were each one for his fathers' house.

45. And all those that were numbered of the children of Israel by their fathers' houses, from twenty years old and upward, all that were able to go forth to war in Israel;

46. Even all those that were numbered were six hundred thousand and three thousand and five hundred and fifty.

47. But the Levites after the tribe of their fathers were not numbered among them.

48. And the LORD spoke unto Moses, saying:

49. Howbeit the tribe of Levi thou shalt not number, neither shalt thou take the sum of them among the children of Israel;

50. But appoint thou the Levites over the tabernacle of the testimony, and over all the furniture thereof, and over all that belongeth to it; they shall bear the tabernacle, and all the furniture thereof; and they shall minister unto it, and shall encamp round about the tabernacle.

51. And when the tabernacle setteth forward, the Levites shall take it down; and when the tabernacle is to be pitched, the Levites shall set it up; and the common man that draweth nigh shall be put to death.

52. And the children of Israel shall pitch their tents, every man with his own camp, and every man with his own standard, according to their hosts.

53. But the Levites shall pitch round about the tabernacle of the testimony, that there be no wrath upon the congregation of the children of Israel; and the Levites shall keep the charge of the tabernacle of the testimony.

54. Thus did the children of Israel; according to all that the LORD commanded Moses, so did they.

Chapter 2

1. And the LORD spoke unto Moses and unto Aaron, saying:

2. The children of Israel shall pitch by their fathers' houses; every man with his own standard, according to the ensigns; a good way off shall they pitch round about the tent of meeting.

3. Now those that pitch on the east side toward the sunrising shall be they of the standard of the camp of Judah, according to their hosts; the prince of the children of Judah being Nahshon the son of Amminadab,

4. And his host, and those that were numbered of them, threescore and fourteen thousand and six hundred;

5. And those that pitch next unto him shall be the tribe of Issachar; the prince of the children of Issachar being Nethanel the son of Zuar,

6. And his host, even those that were numbered thereof, fifty and four thousand and four hundred;

7. And the tribe of Zebulun; the prince of the children of Zebulun being Eliab the son of Helon,

8. And his host, and those that were numbered thereof, fifty and seven thousand and four hundred;

9. All that were numbered of the camp of Judah being a hundred thousand and fourscore thousand and six thousand and four hundred, according to their hosts; they shall set forth first.

10. On the south side shall be the standard of the camp of Reuben according to their hosts; the prince of the children of Reuben being Elizur the son of Shedeur,

11. And his host, and those that were numbered thereof, forty and six thousand and five hundred;

12. And those that pitch next unto him shall be the

tribe of Simeon; the prince of the children of Simeon being Shelumiel the son of Zurishaddai,

13. And his host, and those that were numbered of them, fifty and nine thousand and three hundred;

14. And the tribe of Gad; the prince of the children of Gad being Eliasaph the son of Reuel,

15. And his host, even those that were numbered of them, forty and five thousand and six hundred and fifty;

16. All that were numbered of the camp of Reuben being a hundred thousand and fifty and one thousand and four hundred and fifty, according to their hosts; and they shall set forth second.

17. Then the tent of meeting, with the camp of the Levites, shall set forward in the midst of the camps; as they encamp, so shall they set forward, every man in his place, by their standards.

18. On the west side shall be the standard of the camp of Ephraim according to their hosts; the prince of the children of Ephraim being Elishama the son of Ammihud,

19. And his host, and those that were numbered of them, forty thousand and five hundred;

20. And next unto him shall be the tribe of Manasseh; the prince of the children of Manasseh being Gamaliel the son of Pedahzur,

21. And his host, and those that were numbered of them, thirty and two thousand and two hundred;

22. And the tribe of Benjamin; the prince of the

children of Benjamin being Abidan the son of Gideoni,

23. And his host, and those that were numbered of them, thirty and five thousand and four hundred;

24. All that were numbered of the camp of Ephraim being a hundred thousand and eight thousand and a hundred, according to their hosts; and they shall set forth third.

25. On the north side shall be the standard of the camp of Dan according to their hosts; the prince of the children of Dan being Ahiezer the son of Ammishaddai,

26. And his host, and those that were numbered of them, threescore and two thousand and seven hundred;

27. And those that pitch next unto him shall be the tribe of Asher; the prince of the children of Asher being Pagiel the son of Ochran,

28. And his host, and those that were numbered of them, forty and one thousand and five hundred;

29. And the tribe of Naphtali; the prince of the children of Naphtali being Ahira the son of Enan,

30. And his host, and those that were numbered of them, fifty and three thousand and four hundred;

31. All that were numbered of the camp of Dan being a hundred thousand and fifty and seven thousand and six hundred; they shall set forth Hindmost by their standards.

32. These are they that were numbered of the children

of Israel by their fathers' houses; all that were numbered of the camps according to their hosts were six hundred thousand and three thousand and five hundred and fifty.

33. But the Levites were not numbered among the children of Israel; as the LORD commanded Moses.

34. Thus did the children of Israel: according to all that the LORD commanded Moses, so they pitched by their standards, and so they set forward, each one according to its families, and according to its fathers' houses.

Chapter 3

1. Now these are the generations of Aaron and Moses in the day that the LORD spoke with Moses in mount Sinai.

2. And these are the names of the sons of Aaron: Nadab the first-born, and Abihu, Eleazar, and Ithamar.

3. These are the names of the sons of Aaron, the priests that were anointed, whom he consecrated to minister in the priest's office.

4. And Nadab and Abihu died before the LORD, when they offered strange fire before the LORD, in the wilderness of Sinai, and they had no children; and Eleazar and Ithamar ministered in the priest's office in the presence of Aaron their father.

5. And the LORD spoke unto Moses, saying:

6. Bring the tribe of Levi near, and set them before

Aaron the priest, that they may minister unto him.

7. And they shall keep his charge, and the charge of the whole congregation before the tent of meeting, to do the service of the tabernacle.

8. And they shall keep all the furniture of the tent of meeting, and the charge of the children of Israel, to do the service of the tabernacle.

9. And thou shalt give the Levites unto Aaron and to his sons; they are wholly given unto him from the children of Israel.

10. And thou shalt appoint Aaron and his sons, that they may keep their priesthood; and the common man that draweth nigh shall be put to death.

11. And the LORD spoke unto Moses, saying:

12. And I, behold, I have taken the Levites from among the children of Israel instead of every first-born that openeth the womb among the children of Israel; and the Levites shall be Mine;

13. For all the first-born are Mine: on the day that I smote all the first-born in the land of Egypt I hallowed unto Me all the first-born in Israel, both man and beast, Mine they shall be: I am the LORD.

14. And the LORD spoke unto Moses in the wilderness of Sinai, saying:

15. Number the children of Levi by their fathers' houses, by their families; every male from a month old and upward shalt thou number them.

16. And Moses numbered them according to the word of the LORD, as he was commanded.

17. And these were the sons of Levi by their names: Gershon, and Kohath, and Merari.

18. And these are the names of the sons of Gershon by their families: Libni and Shimei.

19. And the sons of Kohath by their families: Amram and Izhar, Hebron and Uzziel.

20. And the sons of Merari by their families: Mahli and Mushi. These are the families of the Levites according to their fathers' houses.

21. Of Gershon was the family of the Libnites, and the family of the Shimeites; these are the families of the Gershonites.

22. Those that were numbered of them, according to the number of all the males, from a month old and upward, even those that were numbered of them were seven thousand and five hundred.

23. The families of the Gershonites were to pitch beHind the tabernacle westward;

24. The prince of the fathers' house of the Gershonites being Eliasaph the son of Lael,

25. And the charge of the sons of Gershon in the tent of meeting the tabernacle, and the Tent, the covering thereof, and the screen for the door of the tent of meeting,

26. And the hangings of the court, and the screen for the door of the court-which is by the tabernacle, and by the altar, round about-and the cords of it, even whatsoever pertaineth to the service thereof.

27. And of Kohath was the family of the Amramites,

and the family of the Izharites, and the family of the Hebronites, and the family of the Uzzielites; these are the families of the Kohathites:

28. According to the number of all the males, from a month old and upward, eight thousand and six hundred, keepers of the charge of the sanctuary.

29. The families of the sons of Kohath were to pitch on the side of the tabernacle southward;

30. The prince of the fathers' house of the families of the Kohathites being Elizaphan the son of Uzziel,

31. And their charge the ark, and the table, and the candlestick, and the altars, and the vessels of the sanctuary wherewith the priests minister, and the screen, and all that pertaineth to the service thereof;

32. Eleazar the son of Aaron the priest being prince of the princes of the Levites, and having the oversight of them that keep the charge of the sanctuary.

33. Of Merari was the family of the Mahlites, and the family of the Mushites; these are the families of Merari.

34. And those that were numbered of them, according to the number of all the males, from a month old and upward, were six thousand and two hundred;

35. The prince of the fathers' house of the families of Merari being Zuriel the son of Abihail; they were to pitch on the side of the tabernacle northward;

36. The appointed charge of the sons of Merari being the boards of the tabernacle, and the bars thereof, and the pillars thereof, and the sockets thereof, and all the instruments thereof, and all that pertaineth to the service thereof;

37. And the pillars of the court round about, and their sockets, and their pins, and their cords.

38. And those that were to pitch before the tabernacle eastward, before the tent of meeting toward the sunrising, were Moses, and Aaron and his sons, keeping the charge of the sanctuary, even the charge for the children of Israel; and the common man that drew nigh was to be put to death.

39. All that were numbered of the Levites, whom Moses and Aaron numbered at the commandment of the LORD, by their families, all the males from a month old and upward, were twenty and two thousand.

40. And the LORD said unto Moses: Number all the first-born males of the children of Israel from a month old and upward, and take the number of their names.

41. And thou shalt take the Levites for Me, even the LORD, instead of all the first-born among the children of Israel; and the cattle of the Levites instead of all the firstlings among the cattle of the children of Israel.

42. And Moses numbered, as the LORD commanded him, all the first-born among the children of Israel.

43. And all the first-born males according to the number of names, from a month old and upward, of those that were numbered of them, were twenty and two thousand two hundred and threescore and thirteen.

44. And the LORD spoke unto Moses, saying:

45. Take the Levites instead of all the first-born among the children of Israel, and the cattle of the Levites instead of their cattle; and the Levites shall be Mine, even the LORD'S.

46. And as for the redemption of the two hundred and three score and thirteen of the first-born of the children of Israel, that are over and above the number of the Levites,

47. Thou shalt take five shekels apiece by the poll; after the shekel of the sanctuary shalt thou take them- the shekel is twenty gerahs.

48. And thou shalt give the money wherewith they that remain over of them are redeemed unto Aaron and to his sons.

49. And Moses took the redemption-money from them that were over and above them that were redeemed by the Levites;

50. From the first-born of the children of Israel took he the money: a thousand three hundred and threescore and five shekels, after the shekel of the sanctuary.

51. And Moses gave the redemption-money unto Aaron and to his sons, according to the word of the LORD, as the LORD commanded Moses.

Chapter 4

1. And the LORD spoke unto Moses and unto Aaron,

saying:

2. Take the sum of the sons of Kohath from among the sons of Levi, by their families, by their fathers' houses,

3. From thirty years old and upward even until fifty years old, all that enter upon the service, to do work in the tent of meeting.

4. This is the service of the sons of Kohath in the tent of meeting, about the most holy things:

5. When the camp setteth forward, Aaron shall go in, and his sons, and they shall take down the veil of the screen, and cover the ark of the testimony with it;

6. And shall put thereon a covering of sealskin, and shall spread over it a cloth all of blue, and shall set the staves thereof.

7. And upon the table of showbread, they shall spread a cloth of blue, and put thereon the dishes, and the pans, and the bowls, and the jars wherewith to pour out; and the continual bread shall remain thereon.

8. And they shall spread upon them a cloth of scarlet, and cover the same with a covering of sealskin, and shall set the staves thereof.

9. And they shall take a cloth of blue, and cover the candlestick of the light, and its lamps, and its tongs, and its snuffdishes, and all the oil vessels thereof, wherewith they minister unto it.

10. And they shall put it and all the vessels thereof witHin a covering of sealskin, and shall put it upon a bar.

11. And upon the golden altar they shall spread a cloth of blue, and cover it with a covering of sealskin, and shall set the staves thereof.

12. And they shall take all the vessels of ministry, wherewith they minister in the sanctuary, and put them in a cloth of blue, and cover them with a covering of sealskin, and shall put them on a bar.

13. And they shall take away the ashes from the altar, and spread a purple cloth thereon.

14. And they shall put upon it all the vessels thereof, wherewith they minister about it, the fire-pans, the flesh-hooks, and the shovels, and the basins, all the vessels of the altar; and they shall spread upon it a covering of sealskin, and set the staves thereof.

15. And when Aaron and his sons have made an end of covering the holy furniture, and all the holy vessels, as the camp is to set forward-after that, the sons of Kohath shall come to bear them; but they shall not touch the holy things, lest they die. These things are the burden of the sons of Kohath in the tent of meeting.

16. And the charge of Eleazar the son of Aaron the priest shall be the oil for the light, and the sweet incense, and the continual meal-offering, and the anointing oil: he shall have the charge of all the tabernacle, and of all that therein is, whether it be the sanctuary, or the furniture thereof.

17. And the LORD spoke unto Moses and unto Aaron, saying:

18. Cut ye not off the tribe of the families of the Kohathites from among the Levites;

19. But thus, do unto them, that they may live, and not die, when they approach unto the most holy things: Aaron and his sons shall go in, and appoint them every one to his service and to his burden;

20. But they shall not go in to see the holy things as they are being covered, lest they die.

Nasso

21. And the LORD spoke unto Moses saying:

22. Take the sum of the sons of Gershon also, by their fathers' houses, by their families;

23. From thirty years old and upward until fifty years old shalt thou number them: all that enter in to wait upon the service, to do service in the tent of meeting.

24. This is the service of the families of the Gershonites, in serving and in bearing burdens:

25. They shall bear the curtains of the tabernacle, and the tent of meeting, its covering, and the covering of sealskin that is above upon it, and the screen for the door of the tent of meeting;

26. And the hangings of the court, and the screen for the door of the gate of the court, which is by the tabernacle and by the altar round about, and their cords, and all the instruments of their service, and whatsoever there may be to do with them, therein shall they serve.

27. At the commandment of Aaron and his sons shall be all the service of the sons of the Gershonites, in all their burden, and in all their service; and ye shall appoint unto them in charge all their burden.

28. This is the service of the families of the sons of the Gershonites in the tent of meeting; and their charge shall be under the hand of Ithamar the son of Aaron the priest.

29. As for the sons of Merari, thou shalt number them by their families, by their fathers' houses;

30. From thirty years old and upward even unto fifty years old shalt thou number them, every one that entereth upon the service, to do the work of the tent of meeting.

31. And this is the charge of their burden, according to all their service in the tent of meeting: the boards of the tabernacle, and the bars thereof, and the pillars thereof, and the sockets thereof;

32. And the pillars of the court round about, and their sockets, and their pins, and their cords, even all their appurtenance, and all that pertaineth to their service; and by name ye shall appoint the instruments of the charge of their burden.

33. This is the service of the families of the sons of Merari, according to all their service, in the tent of meeting, under the hand of Ithamar the son of Aaron the priest.

34. And Moses and Aaron and the princes of the congregation numbered the sons of the Kohathites by their families, and by their fathers' houses,

35. From thirty years old and upward even unto fifty years old, every one that entered upon the service, for service in the tent of meeting.

36. And those that were numbered of them by their families were two thousand seven hundred and fifty.

37. These are they that were numbered of the families of the Kohathites, of all that did serve in the tent of meeting, whom Moses and Aaron numbered according to the commandment of the LORD by the hand of Moses.

38. And those that were numbered of the sons of Gershon, by their families, and by their fathers' houses,

39. From thirty years old and upward even unto fifty years old, every one that entered upon the service, for service in the tent of meeting,

40. Even those that were numbered of them, by their families, by their fathers' houses, were two thousand and six hundred and thirty.

41. These are they that were numbered of the families of the sons of Gershon, of all that did serve in the tent of meeting, whom Moses and Aaron numbered according to the commandment of the LORD.

42. And those that were numbered of the families of the sons of Merari, by their families, by their fathers' houses,

43. From thirty years old and upward even unto fifty years old, every one that entered upon the service, for service in the tent of meeting,

44. Even those that were numbered of them by their families, were three thousand and two hundred.

45. These are they that were numbered of the families of the sons of Merari, whom Moses and Aaron numbered according to the commandment of the LORD by the hand of Moses.

46. All those that were numbered of the Levites, whom Moses and Aaron and the princes of Israel numbered, by their families, and by their fathers' houses,

47. From thirty years old and upward even unto fifty years old, every one that entered in to do the work of service, and the work of bearing burdens in the tent of meeting,

48. Even those that were numbered of them, were eight thousand and five hundred and fourscore.

49. According to the commandment of the LORD they were appointed by the hand of Moses, every one to his service, and to his burden; they were also numbered, as the LORD commanded Moses.

Chapter 5

1. And the LORD spoke unto Moses, saying:

2. Command the children of Israel, that they put out of the camp every leper, and every one that hath an issue, and whosoever is unclean by the dead;

3. Both male and female shall ye put out, without the camp shall ye put them; that they defile not their camp, in the midst whereof I dwell.

4. And the children of Israel did so, and put them out without the camp; as the LORD spoke unto Moses, so did the children of Israel.

5. And the LORD spoke unto Moses, saying:

6. Speak unto the children of Israel: When a man or woman shall commit any sin that men commit, to commit a trespass against the LORD, and that soul be guilty;

7. Then they shall confess their sin which they have done; and he shall make restitution for his guilt in full, and add unto it the fifth part thereof, and give it unto him in respect of whom he hath been guilty.

8. But if the man have no kinsman to whom restitution may be made for the guilt, the restitution for guilt which is made shall be the LORD'S, even the priest's; besides the ram of the atonement, whereby atonement shall be made for him.

9. And every heave-offering of all the holy things of the children of Israel, which they present unto the priest, shall be his.

10. And every man's hallowed things shall be his: whatsoever any man giveth the priest, it shall be his.

11. And the LORD spoke unto Moses, saying:

12. Speak unto the children of Israel, and say unto them: If any man's wife go aside, and act unfaithfully against him,

13. And a man lie with her carnally, and it be hid from the eyes of her husband, she being defiled secretly, and there be no witness against her, neither she be taken in the act;

14. And the spirit of jealousy come upon him, and he warned his wife, and she be defiled; or if the spirit of jealousy come upon him, and he warned his wife, and she be not defiled;

15. Then shall the man bring his wife unto the priest, and shall bring her offering for her, the tenth part of an ephah of barley meal; he shall pour no oil upon it, nor put frankincense thereon; for it is a meal-offering of jealousy, a meal-offering of memorial, bringing iniquity to remembrance.

16. And the priest shall bring her near, and set her before the LORD.

17. And the priest shall take holy water in an earthen vessel; and of the dust that is on the floor of the tabernacle the priest shall take, and put it into the water.

18. And the priest shall set the woman before the LORD, and let the hair of the woman's head go loose, and put the meal-offering of memorial in her hands, which is the meal-offering of jealousy; and the priest shall have in his hand the water of bitterness that causeth the curse.

19. And the priest shall cause her to swear, and shall say unto the woman: If no man have lain with thee, and if thou hast not gone aside to uncleanness, being under thy husband, be thou free from this water of bitterness that causeth the curse;

20. But if thou hast gone aside, being under thy husband, and if thou be defiled, and some man have lain with thee besides thy husband.

21. Then the priest shall cause the woman to swear with the oath of cursing, and the priest shall say unto the woman-the LORD make thee a curse and an oath among thy people, when the LORD doth make thy thigh to fall away, and thy belly to swell;

22. And this water that causeth the curse shall go into thy bowels, and make thy belly to swell, and thy thigh to fall away; and the woman shall say: Amen, Amen.

23. And the priest shall write these curses in a scroll, and he shall blot them out into the water of bitterness.

24. And he shall make the woman drink the water of bitterness that causeth the curse; and the water that causeth the curse shall enter into her and become bitter.

25. And the priest shall take the meal-offering of jealousy out of the woman's hand, and shall wave the meal-offering before the LORD, and bring it unto the altar.

26. And the priest shall take a handful of the meal-offering, as the memorial-part thereof, and make it smoke upon the altar, and afterward shall make the woman drink the water.

27. And when he hath made her drink the water, then it shall come to pass, if she be defiled, and have acted unfaithfully against her husband, that the water that causeth the curse shall enter into her and become bitter, and her belly shall swell, and her thigh shall fall away; and the woman shall be a curse among her people.

28. And if the woman be not defiled, but be clean; then she shall be cleared, and shall conceive seed.

29. This is the law of jealousy, when a wife, being under her husband, goeth aside, and is defiled;

30. Or when the spirit of jealousy cometh upon a man, and he be jealous over his wife; then shall he set the woman before the LORD, and the priest shall execute upon her all this law.

31. And the man shall be clear from iniquity, and that woman shall bear her iniquity.

Chapter 6

1. And the LORD spoke unto Moses, saying:

2. Speak unto the children of Israel, and say unto them: When either man or woman shall clearly utter a vow, the vow of a Nazirite, to consecrate himself unto the LORD,

3. He shall abstain from wine and strong drink: he shall drink no vinegar of wine, or vinegar of strong drink, neither shall he drink any liquor of grapes, nor eat fresh grapes or dried.

4. All the days of his Naziriteship shall he eat nothing that is made of the grape-vine, from the pressed grapes even to the grapestone.

5. All the days of his vow of Naziriteship there shall no razor come upon his head; until the days be fulfilled, in which he consecrateth himself unto the LORD, he shall be holy, he shall let the locks of the hair of his head grow long.

6. All the days that he consecrateth himself unto the LORD he shall not come near to a dead body.

7. He shall not make himself unclean for his father, or for his mother, for his brother, or for his sister, when they die; because his consecration unto God is upon his head.

8. All the days of his Naziriteship he is holy unto the LORD.

9. And if any man die very suddenly beside him, and he defile his consecrated head, then he shall shave his head in the day of his cleansing, on the seventh day shall he shave it.

10. And on the eighth day he shall bring two turtledoves, or two young pigeons, to the priest, to the door of the tent of meeting.

11. And the priest shall prepare one for a sin-offering, and the other for a burnt-offering, and make atonement for him, for that he sinned by reason of the dead; and he shall hallow his head that same day.

12. And he shall consecrate unto the LORD the days of his Naziriteship, and shall bring a he-lamb of the first year for a guilt-offering; but the former days shall be void, because his consecration was defiled.

13. And this is the law of the Nazirite, when the days of his consecration are fulfilled: he shall abring it unto the door of the tent of meeting;

14. And he shall present his offering unto the LORD, one he-lamb of the first year without blemish for a burnt-offering, and one ewe-lamb of the first year without blemish for a sin-offering, and one ram without blemish for peace-offerings,

15. And a basket of unleavened bread, cakes of fine flour mingled with oil, and unleavened wafers spread with oil, and their meal-offering, and their drink-offerings.

16. And the priest shall bring them before the LORD, and shall offer his sin-offering, and his burnt-offering.

17. And he shall offer the ram for a sacrifice of peace-offerings unto the LORD, with the basket of unleavened bread; the priest shall offer also the meal-offering thereof, and the drink-offering thereof.

18. And the Nazirite shall shave his consecrated head at the door of the tent of meeting, and shall take the hair of his consecrated head, and put it on the fire which is under the sacrifice of peace-offerings.

19. And the priest shall take the shoulder of the ram when it is sodden, and one unleavened cake out of the basket, and one unleavened wafer, and shall put them upon the hands of the Nazirite, after he hath shaven his consecrated head.

20. And the priest shall wave them for a wave-offering before the LORD; this is holy for the priest, together with the breast of waving and the thigh of heaving; and after that the Nazirite may drink wine.

21. This is the law of the Nazirite who voweth, and of his offering unto the LORD for his Naziriteship, beside that for which his means suffice; according to his vow which he voweth, so he must do after the law of his Naziriteship.

22. And the LORD spoke unto Moses, saying:

23. Speak unto Aaron and unto his sons, saying: On this wise ye shall bless the children of Israel; ye shall say unto them:

24. The LORD bless thee, and keep thee;

25. The LORD make His face to sHine upon thee, and be gracious unto thee;

26. The LORD lift up His countenance upon thee, and give thee peace.

27. So shall they put My name upon the children of Israel, and I will bless them.

Chapter 7

1. And it came to pass on the day that Moses had made an end of setting up the tabernacle, and had anointed it and sanctified it, and all the furniture thereof, and the altar and all the vessels thereof, and had anointed them and sanctified them;

2. That the princes of Israel, the heads of their fathers' houses, offered-these were the princes of the tribes, these are they that were over them that were numbered.

3. And they brought their offering before the LORD, six covered wagons, and twelve oxen: a wagon for every two of the princes, and for each one an ox; and they presented them before the tabernacle.

4. And the LORD spoke unto Moses, saying:

5. Take it of them, that they may be to do the service of the tent of meeting; and thou shalt give them unto the Levites, to every man according to his service.

6. And Moses took the wagons and the oxen, and gave them unto the Levites.

7. Two wagons and four oxen he gave unto the sons of Gershon, according to their service.

8. And four wagons and eight oxen he gave unto the sons of Merari, according unto their service, under the hand of Ithamar the son of Aaron the priest.

9. But unto the sons of Kohath, he gave none, because the service of the holy things belonged unto them: they bore them upon their shoulders.

10. And the princes brought the dedication-offering of the altar in the day that it was anointed, even the princes brought their offering before the altar.

11. And the LORD said unto Moses: They shall present their offering each prince on his day, for the dedication of the altar.

12. And he that presented his offering the first day was Nahshon the son of Amminadab, of the tribe of Judah;

13. And his offering was one silver dish, the weight thereof was a hundred and thirty shekels, one silver basin of seventy shekels, after the shekel of the sanctuary; both of them full of fine flour mingled with oil for a meal-offering;

14. One golden pan of ten shekels, full of incense;

15. One young bullock, one ram, one he-lamb of the first year, for a burnt-offering;

16. One male of the goats for a sin-offering;

17. And for the sacrifice of peace-offerings, two oxen, five rams, five he-goats, five he-lambs of the first year. This was the offering of Nahshon the son of Amminadab.

18. On the second day Nethanel the son of Zuar, prince of Issachar, did offer:

19. He presented for his offering one silver dish, the weight thereof was a hundred and thirty shekels, one silver basin of seventy shekels, after the shekel of the sanctuary; both of them full of fine flour mingled with oil for a meal-offering;

20. One golden pan of ten shekels, full of incense;

21. One young bullock, one ram, one he-lamb of the first year, for a burnt-offering;

22. One male of the goats for a sin-offering;

23. And for the sacrifice of peace-offerings, two oxen, five rams, five he-goats, five he-lambs of the first year. This was the offering of Nethanel the son of Zuar.

24. On the third day Eliab the son of Helon, prince of the children of Zebulun:

25. His offering was one silver dish, the weight thereof was a hundred and thirty shekels, one silver basin of seventy shekels, after the shekel of the sanctuary; both of them full of fine flour mingled with oil for a meal-offering;

26. One golden pan of ten shekels, full of incense;

27. One young bullock, one ram, one he-lamb of the first year, for a burnt-offering;

28. One male of the goats for a sin-offering;

29. And for the sacrifice of peace-offerings, two oxen, five rams, five he-goats, five he-lambs of the first year. This was the offering of Eliab the son of Helon.

30. On the fourth day Elizur the son of Shedeur, prince of the children of Reuben:

31. His offering was one silver dish, the weight thereof was a hundred and thirty shekels, one silver basin of seventy shekels, after the shekel of the sanctuary; both of them full of fine flour mingled with oil for a meal-offering;

32. One golden pan of ten shekels, full of incense;

33. One young bullock, one ram, one he-lamb of the first year, for a burnt-offering;

34. One male of the goats for a sin-offering;

35. And for the sacrifice of peace-offerings, two oxen, five rams, five he-goats, five he-lambs of the first year. This was the offering of Elizur the son of Shedeur.

36. On the fifth day Shelumiel the son of Zurishaddai, prince of the children of Simeon:

37. His offering was one silver dish, the weight thereof was a hundred and thirty shekels, one silver basin of seventy shekels, after the shekel of the sanctuary; both of them full of fine flour mingled with oil for a meal-offering;

38. One golden pan of ten shekels, full of incense;

39. One young bullock, one ram, one he-lamb of the first year, for a burnt-offering;

40. One male of the goats for a sin-offering;

41. And for the sacrifice of peace-offerings, two oxen, five rams, five he-goats, five he-lambs of the first year. This was the offering of Shelumiel the son of Zurishaddai.

42. On the sixth day Eliasaph the son of Deuel, prince of the children of Gad:

43. His offering was one silver dish, the weight thereof was a hundred and thirty shekels, one silver basin of seventy shekels, after the shekel of the sanctuary; both of them full of fine flour mingled with oil for a meal-offering;

44. One golden pan of ten shekels, full of incense;

45. One young bullock, one ram, one he-lamb of the first year, for a burnt-offering;

46. One male of the goats for a sin-offering;

47. And for the sacrifice of peace-offerings, two oxen, five rams, five he-goats, five he-lambs of the first year. This was the offering of Eliasaph the son of Deuel.

48. On the seventh day Elishama the son of Ammihud, prince of the children of Ephraim:

49. His offering was one silver dish, the weight

thereof was a hundred and thirty shekels, one silver basin of seventy shekels, after the shekel of the sanctuary; both of them full of fine flour mingled with oil for a meal-offering;

50. One golden pan of ten shekels, full of incense;

51. One young bullock, one ram, one he-lamb of the first year, for a burnt-offering;

52. One male of the goats for a sin-offering;

53. And for the sacrifice of peace-offerings, two oxen, five rams, five he-goats, five he-lambs of the first year. This was the offering of Elishama the son of Ammihud.

54. On the eighth day Gamaliel the son of Pedahzur, prince of the children of Manasseh:

55. His offering was one silver dish, the weight thereof was a hundred and thirty shekels, one silver basin of seventy shekels, after the shekel of the sanctuary; both of them full of fine flour mingled with oil for a meal-offering;

56. One golden pan of ten shekels, full of incense;

57. One young bullock, one ram, one he-lamb of the first year, for a burnt-offering;

58. One male of the goats for a sin-offering;

59. And for the sacrifice of peace-offerings, two oxen, five rams, five he-goats, five he-lamb of the first year. This was the offering of Gamaliel the son of Pedahzur.

60. On the ninth day Abidan the son of Gideoni, prince of the children of Benjamin:

61. His offering was one silver dish, the weight thereof was a hundred and thirty shekels, one silver basin of seventy shekels, after the shekel of the sanctuary; both of them full of fine flour mingled with oil for a meal-offering;

62. One golden pan of ten shekels, full of incense;

63. One young bullock, one ram, one he-lamb of the first year, for a burnt-offering;

64. One male of the goats for a sin-offering;

65. And for the sacrifice of peace-offerings, two oxen, five rams, five he-goats, five he-lambs of the first year. This was the offering of Abidan the son of Gideoni.

66. On the tenth day Ahiezer the son of Ammishaddai, prince of the children of Dan:

67. His offering was one silver dish, the weight thereof was a hundred and thirty shekels, one silver basin of seventy shekels, after the shekel of the sanctuary; both of them full of fine flour mingled with oil for a meal-offering;

68. One golden pan of ten shekels, full of incense;

69. One young bullock, one ram, one he-lamb of the first year, for a burnt-offering;

70. One male of the goats for a sin-offering;

71. And for the sacrifice of peace-offerings, two oxen, five rams, five he-goats, five he-lambs of the first year. This was the offering of Ahiezer the son of Ammishaddai.

72. On the eleventh day Pagiel the son of Ochran,

prince of the children of Asher:

73. His offering was one silver dish, the weight thereof was a hundred and thirty shekels, one silver basin of seventy shekels, after the shekel of the sanctuary; both of them full of fine flour mingled with oil for a meal-offering;

74. One golden pan of ten shekels, full of incense;

75. One young bullock, one ram, one he-lamb of the first year, for a burnt-offering;

76. One male of the goats for a sin-offering;

77. And for the sacrifice of peace-offerings, two oxen, five rams, five he-goats, five he-lambs of the first year. This was the offering of Pagiel the son of Ochran.

78. On the twelfth day Ahira the son of Enan, prince of the children of Naphtali:

79. His offering was one silver dish, the weight thereof was a hundred and thirty shekels, one silver basin of seventy shekels, after the shekel of the sanctuary; both of them full of fine flour mingled with oil for a meal-offering;

80. One golden pan of ten shekels, full of incense;

81. One young bullock, one ram, one he-lamb of the first year, for a burnt-offering;

82. One male of the goats for a sin-offering;

83. And for the sacrifice of peace-offerings, two oxen, five rams, five he-goats, five he-lambs of the first year. This was the offering of Ahira the son of Enan.

84. This was the dedication-offering of the altar, in the day when it was anointed, at the hands of the princes of Israel: twelve silver dishes, twelve silver basins, twelve golden pans;

85. Each silver dish weigHing a hundred and thirty shekels, and each basin seventy; all the silver of the vessels two thousand and four hundred shekels, after the shekel of the sanctuary;

86. Twelve golden pans, full of incense, weigHing ten shekels apiece, after the shekel of the sanctuary; all the gold of the pans a hundred and twenty shekels;

87. All the oxen for the burnt-offering twelve bullocks, the rams twelve, the he-lambs of the first year twelve, and their meal-offering; and the males of the goats for a sin-offering twelve;

88. And all the oxen for the sacrifice of peace-offerings twenty and four bullocks, the rams sixty, the he-goats sixty, the he-lambs of the first year sixty. This was the dedication-offering of the altar, after that it was anointed.

89. And when Moses went into the tent of meeting that He might speak with him, then he heard the Voice speaking unto him from above the ark-cover that was upon the ark of the testimony, from between the two cherubim; and He spoke unto him.

Beha'alotcha

Chapter 8

1. And the LORD spoke unto Moses, saying:

2. Speak unto Aaron, and say unto him: When thou lightest the lamps, the seven lamps shall give light in front of the candlestick.

3. And Aaron did so: he lighted the lamps thereof so as to give light in front of the candlestick, as the LORD commanded Moses.

4. And this was the work of the candlestick, beaten work of gold; unto the base thereof, and unto the flowers thereof, it was beaten work; according unto the pattern which the LORD had shown Moses, so he made the candlestick.

5. And the LORD spoke unto Moses, saying:

6. Take the Levites from among the children of Israel, and cleanse them.

7. And thus, shalt thou do unto them, to cleanse them: sprinkle the water of purification upon them, and let them cause a razor to pass over all their flesh, and let them wash their clothes, and cleanse themselves.

8. Then let them take a young bullock, and its meal-offering, fine flour mingled with oil, and another young bullock shalt thou take for a sin-offering.

9. And thou shalt present the Levites before the tent of meeting; and thou shalt assemble the whole congregation of the children of Israel.

10. And thou shalt present the Levites before the LORD; and the children of Israel shall lay their hands upon the Levites.

11. And Aaron shall offer the Levites before the LORD for a wave-offering from the children of

Israel, that they may be to do the service of the LORD.

12. And the Levites shall lay their hands upon the heads of the bullocks; and offer thou the one for a sin-offering, and the other for a burnt-offering, unto the LORD, to make atonement for the Levites.

13. And thou shalt set the Levites before Aaron, and before his sons, and offer them for a wave-offering unto the LORD.

14. Thus, shalt thou separate the Levites from among the children of Israel; and the Levites shall be Mine.

15. And after that shall the Levites go in to do the service of the tent of meeting; and thou shalt cleanse them, and offer them for a wave-offering.

16. For they are wholly given unto Me from among the children of Israel; instead of all that openeth the womb, even the first-born of all the children of Israel, have I taken them unto Me.

17. For all the first-born among the children of Israel are Mine, both man and beast; on the day that I smote all the first-born in the land of Egypt I sanctified them for Myself.

18. And I have taken the Levites instead of all the first-born among the children of Israel.

19. And I have given the Levites - they are given to Aaron and to his sons from among the children of Israel, to do the service of the children of Israel in the tent of meeting, and to make atonement for the children of Israel, that there be no plague among the children of Israel, through the children of Israel coming nigh unto the sanctuary.

20. Thus did Moses, and Aaron, and all the congregation of the children of Israel, unto the Levites; according unto all that the LORD commanded Moses toucHing the Levites, so did the children of Israel unto them.

21. And the Levites purified themselves, and they washed their clothes; and Aaron offered them for a sacred gift before the LORD; and Aaron made atonement for them to cleanse them.

22. And after that went the Levites in to do their service in the tent of meeting before Aaron, and before his sons; as the LORD had commanded Moses concerning the Levites, so did they unto them.

23. And the LORD spoke unto Moses, saying:

24. This is that which pertaineth unto the Levites: from twenty and five years old and upward they shall go in to perform the service in the work of the tent of meeting;

25. And from the age of fifty years, they shall return from the service of the work, and shall serve no more;

26. But shall minister with their brethren in the tent of meeting, to keep the charge, but they shall do no manner of service. Thus, shalt thou do unto the Levites toucHing their charges.

Chapter 9

1. And the LORD spoke unto Moses in the wilderness

of Sinai, in the first month of the second year after they were come out of the land of Egypt, saying:

2. Let the children of Israel keep the Passover in its appointed season.

3. In the fourteenth day of this month, at dusk, ye shall keep it in its appointed season; according to all the statutes of it, and according to all the ordinances thereof, shall ye keep it.

4. And Moses spoke unto the children of Israel, that they should keep the Passover.

5. And they kept the Passover in the first month, on the fourteenth day of the month, at dusk, in the wilderness of Sinai; according to all that the LORD commanded Moses, so did the children of Israel.

6. But there were certain men, who were unclean by the dead body of a man, so that they could not keep the Passover on that day; and they came before Moses and before Aaron on that day.

7. And those men said unto him: We are unclean by the dead body of a man; wherefore are we to be kept back, so as not to bring the offering of the LORD in its appointed season among the children of Israel.

8. And Moses said unto them: Stay ye, that I may hear what the LORD will command concerning you.

9. And the LORD spoke unto Moses, saying:

10. Speak unto the children of Israel, saying: If any man of you or of your generations shall be unclean by reason of a dead body, or be in a journey afar off, yet he shall keep the Passover unto the LORD;

11. In the second month on the fourteenth day at dusk they shall keep it; they shall eat it with unleavened bread and bitter herbs;

12. They shall leave none of it unto the morning, nor break a bone thereof; according to all the statute of the Passover they shall keep it.

13. But the man that is clean, and is not on a journey, and forbeareth to keep the Passover, that soul shall be cut off from his people; because he brought not the offering of the LORD in its appointed season, that man shall bear his sin.

14. And if a stranger shall sojourn among you, and will keep the Passover unto the LORD: according to the statute of the Passover, and according to the ordinance thereof, so shall he do; ye shall have one statute, both for the stranger, and for him that is born in the land.

15. And on the day that the tabernacle was reared up the cloud covered the tabernacle, even the tent of the testimony; and at even there was upon the tabernacle as it were the appearance of fire, until morning.

16. So, it was alway: the cloud covered it, and the appearance of fire by night.

17. And whenever the cloud was taken up from over the Tent, then after that the children of Israel journeyed; and in the place where the cloud abode, there the children of Israel encamped.

18. At the commandment of the LORD the children of Israel journeyed, and at the commandment of the

LORD they encamped: as long as the cloud abode upon the tabernacle they remained encamped.

19. And when the cloud tarried upon the tabernacle many days, then the children of Israel kept the charge of the LORD, and journeyed not.

20. And sometimes the cloud was a few days upon the tabernacle; according to the commandment of the LORD they remained encamped, and according to the commandment of the LORD they journeyed.

21. And sometimes the cloud was from evening until morning; and when the cloud was taken up in the morning, they journeyed; or if it continued by day and by night, when the cloud was taken up, they journeyed.

22. Whether it were two days, or a month, or a year, that the cloud tarried upon the tabernacle, abiding thereon, the children of Israel remained encamped, and journeyed not; but when it was taken up, they journeyed.

23. At the commandment of the LORD, they encamped, and at the commandment of the LORD they journeyed; they kept the charge of the LORD, at the commandment of the LORD by the hand of Moses.

Chapter 10

1. And the LORD spoke unto Moses, saying:

2. Make thee two trumpets of silver; of beaten work shalt thou make them; and they shall be unto thee for the calling of the congregation, and for causing the camps to set forward.

3. And when they shall blow with them, all the congregation shall gather themselves unto thee at the door of the tent of meeting.

4. And if they blow but with one, then the princes, the heads of the thousands of Israel, shall gather themselves unto thee.

5. And when ye blow an alarm, the camps that lie on the east side shall take their journey.

6. And when ye blow an alarm the second time, the camps that lie on the south side shall set forward; they shall blow an alarm for their journeys.

7. But when the assembly is to be gathered together, ye shall blow, but ye shall not sound an alarm.

8. And the sons of Aaron, the priests, shall blow with the trumpets; and they shall be to you for a statute for ever throughout your generations.

9. And when ye go to war in your land against the adversary that oppresseth you, then ye shall sound an alarm with the trumpets; and ye shall be remembered before the LORD your God, and ye shall be saved from your enemies.

10. Also, in the day of your gladness, and in your appointed seasons, and in your new moons, ye shall blow with the trumpets over your burnt-offerings, and over the sacrifices of your peace-offerings; and they shall be to you for a memorial before your God: I am the LORD your God.

11. And it came to pass in the second year, in the second month, on the twentieth day of the month, that the cloud was taken up from over the tabernacle of the testimony.

12. And the children of Israel set forward by their stages out of the wilderness of Sinai; and the cloud abode in the wilderness of Paran.

13. And they took their first journey, according to the commandment of the LORD by the hand of Moses.

14. And in the first place the standard of the camp of the children of Judah set forward according to their hosts; and over his host was Nahshon the son of Amminadab.

15. And over the host of the tribe of the children of Issachar was Nethanel the son of Zuar.

16. And over the host of the tribe of the children of Zebulun was Eliab the son of Helon.

17. And the tabernacle was taken down; and the sons of Gershon and the sons of Merari, who bore the tabernacle, set forward.

18. And the standard of the camp of Reuben set forward according to their hosts; and over his host was Elizur the son of Shedeur.

19. And over the host of the tribe of the children of Simeon was Shelumiel the son of Zurishaddai.

20. And over the host of the tribe of the children of Gad was Eliasaph the son of Deuel.

21. And the Kohathites the bearers of the sanctuary set forward, that the tabernacle might be set up against their coming.

22. And the standard of the camp of the children of Ephraim set forward according to their hosts; and over his host was Elishama the son of Ammihud.

23. And over the host of the tribe of the children of Manasseh was Gamaliel the son of Pedahzur.

24. And over the host of the tribe of the children of Benjamin was Abidan the son of Gideoni.

25. And the standard of the camp of the children of Dan, which was the rearward of all the camps, set forward according to their hosts; and over his host was Ahiezer the son of Ammishaddai.

26. And over the host of the tribe of the children of Asher was Pagiel the son of Ochran.

27. And over the host of the tribe of the children of Naphtali was Ahira the son of Enan.

28. Thus were the journeyings of the children of Israel according to their hosts. And they set forward.

29. And Moses said unto Hobab, the son of Reuel the Midianite, Moses' father-in-law: We are journeying unto the place of which the LORD said: I will give it you; come thou with us, and we will do thee good; for the LORD hath spoken good concerning Israel.

30. And he said unto him: I will not go; but I will depart to mine own land, and to my kindred.

31. And he said: Leave us not, I pray thee; forasmuch as thou knowest how we are to encamp in the wilderness, and thou shalt be to us instead of eyes.

32. And it shall be, if thou go with us, yea, it shall be, that what good soever the LORD shall do unto us, the same will we do unto thee.

33. And they set forward from the mount of the LORD three days' journey; and the ark of the covenant of the LORD went before them three days' journey, to seek out a resting-place for them.

34. And the cloud of the LORD was over them by day, when they set forward from the camp.

35. And it came to pass, when the ark set forward, that Moses said: Rise up, O LORD, and let Thine enemies be scattered; and let them that hate Thee flee before Thee.

36. And when it rested, he said: Return, O LORD, unto the ten thousands of the families of Israel.

Chapter 11

1. And the people were as murmurers, speaking evil in the ears of the LORD; and when the LORD heard it, His anger was kindled; and the fire of the LORD burnt among them, and devoured in the uttermost part of the camp.

2. And the people cried unto Moses; and Moses prayed unto the LORD, and the fire abated.

3. And the name of that place was called Taberah, because the fire of the LORD burnt among them.

4. And the mixed multitude that was among them fell a lusting; and the children of Israel also wept on their part, and said: Would that we were given flesh to eat!

5. We remember the fish, which we were wont to eat

in Egypt for nought; the cucumbers, and the melons, and the leeks, and the onions, and the garlic;

6. But now our soul is dried away; there is nothing at all; we have nought save this manna to look to.

7. Now the manna was like coriander seed, and the appearance thereof as the appearance of bdellium.

8. The people went about, and gathered it, and ground it in mills, or beat it in mortars, and seethed it in pots, and made cakes of it; and the taste of it was as the taste of a cake baked with oil.

9. And when the dew fell upon the camp in the night, the manna fell upon it.

10. And Moses heard the people weeping, family by family, every man at the door of his tent; and the anger of the LORD was kindled greatly; and Moses was displeased.

11. And Moses said unto the LORD: Wherefore hast Thou dealt ill with Thy servant? and wherefore have I not found favour in Thy sight, that Thou layest the burden of all this people upon me?

12. Have I conceived all this people? have I brought them forth, that Thou shouldest say unto me: Carry them in thy bosom, as a nursing-father carrieth the sucking child, unto the land which Thou didst swear unto their fathers.

13. Whence should I have flesh to give unto all this people? for they trouble me with their weeping, saying: Give us flesh, that we may eat.

14. I am not able to bear all this people myself alone,

because it is too heavy for me.

15. And if Thou deal thus with me, kill me, I pray Thee, out of hand, if I have found favour in Thy sight; and let me not look upon my wretchedness.

16. And the LORD said unto Moses: Gather unto Me seventy men of the elders of Israel, whom thou knowest to be the elders of the people, and officers over them; and bring them unto the tent of meeting, that they may stand there with thee.

17. And I will come down and speak with thee there; and I will take of the spirit which is upon thee, and will put it upon them; and they shall bear the burden of the people with thee, that thou bear it not thyself alone.

18. And say thou unto the people: Sanctify yourselves against to-morrow, and ye shall eat flesh; for ye have wept in the ears of the LORD, saying: Would that we were given flesh to eat! for it was well with us in Egypt; therefore, the LORD will give you flesh, and ye shall eat.

19. Ye shall not eat one day, nor two days, nor five days, neither ten days, nor twenty days;

20. But a whole month, until it come out at your nostrils, and it be loathsome unto you; because that ye have rejected the LORD who is among you, and have troubled Him with weeping, saying: Why, now, came we forth out of Egypt.

21. And Moses said: The people, among whom I am, are six hundred thousand men on foot; and yet Thou hast said: I will give them flesh, that they may eat a whole month.

22. If flocks and herds be slain for them, will they suffice them? or if all the fish of the sea be gathered together for them, will they suffice them.

23. And the LORD said unto Moses: Is the LORD'S hand waxed short? now shalt thou see whether My word shall come to pass unto thee or not.

24. And Moses went out, and told the people the words of the LORD; and he gathered seventy men of the elders of the people, and set them round about the Tent.

25. And the LORD came down in the cloud, and spoke unto him, and took of the spirit that was upon him, and put it upon the seventy elders; and it came to pass, that, when the spirit rested upon them, they prophesied, but they did so no more.

26. But there remained two men in the camp, the name of the one was Eldad, and the name of the other Medad; and the spirit rested upon them; and they were of them that were recorded, but had not gone out unto the Tent; and they prophesied in the camp.

27. And there ran a young man, and told Moses, and said: Eldad and Medad are prophesying in the camp.

28. And Joshua the son of Nun, the minister of Moses from his youth up, answered and said: My lord Moses, shut them in.

29. And Moses said unto him: Art thou jealous for my sake? would that all the LORD'S people were prophets, that the LORD would put His spirit upon them.

30. And Moses withdrew into the camp, he and the elders of Israel.

31. And there went forth a wind from the LORD, and brought across quails from the sea, and let them fall by the camp, about a day's journey on this side, and a day's journey on the other side, round about the camp, and about two cubits above the face of the earth.

32. And the people rose up all that day, and all the night, and all the next day, and gathered the quails; he that gathered least gathered ten heaps; and they spread them all abroad for themselves round about the camp.

33. While the flesh was yet between their teeth, ere it was chewed, the anger of the LORD was kindled against the people, and the LORD smote the people with a very great plague.

34. And the name of that place was called Kibroth-hattaavah, because there they buried the people that lusted.

35. From Kibroth-hattaavah the people journeyed unto Hazeroth; and they abode at Hazeroth.

Chapter 12

1. And Miriam and Aaron spoke against Moses because of the Cushite [Black] woman whom he had married; for he had married a Cushite woman.

2. And they said: Hath the LORD indeed spoken only with Moses? hath He not spoken also with us. And the LORD heard it.

3. Now the man Moses was very meek, above all the men that were upon the face of the earth.

4. And the LORD spoke suddenly unto Moses, and unto Aaron, and unto Miriam: Come out ye three unto the tent of meeting. And they three came out.

5. And the LORD came down in a pillar of cloud, and stood at the door of the Tent, and called Aaron and Miriam; and they both came forth.

6. And He said: Hear now My words: if there be a prophet among you, I the LORD do make Myself known unto him in a vision, I do speak with him in a dream.

7. My servant Moses is not so; he is trusted in all My house;

8. With him do I speak mouth to mouth, even manifestly, and not in dark speeches; and the similitude of the LORD doth he behold; wherefore then were ye not afraid to speak against My servant, against Moses.

9. And the anger of the LORD was kindled against them; and He departed.

10. And when the cloud was removed from over the Tent, behold, Miriam was leprous, as white as snow; and Aaron looked upon Miriam; and, behold, she was leprous.

11. And Aaron said unto Moses: Oh, my lord, lay not,

I pray thee, sin upon us, for that we have done foolishly, and for that we have sinned.

12. Let her not, I pray, be as one dead, of whom the flesh is half consumed when he cometh out of his mother's womb.

13. And Moses cried unto the LORD, saying: Heal her now, O God, I beseech Thee.

14. And the LORD said unto Moses: If her father had but spit in her face, should she not hide in shame seven days? let her be shut up without the camp seven days, and after that she shall be brought in again.

15. And Miriam was shut up without the camp seven days; and the people journeyed not till Miriam was brought in again.

16. And afterward the people journeyed from Hazeroth, and pitched in the wilderness of Paran.

Sh'lach

Chapter 13

1. And the LORD spoke unto Moses, saying:

2. Send thou men, that they may spy out the land of Canaan, which I give unto the children of Israel; of every tribe of their fathers shall ye send a man, every one a prince among them.

3. And Moses sent them from the wilderness of Paran according to the commandment of the LORD; all of them men who were heads of the children of Israel.

4. And these were their names: of the tribe of Reuben, Shammua the son of Zaccur.

5. Of the tribe of Simeon, Shaphat the son of Hori.

6. Of the tribe of Judah, Caleb the son of Jephunneh.

7. Of the tribe of Issachar, Igal the son of Joseph.

8. Of the tribe of Ephraim, Hoshea the son of Nun.

9. Of the tribe of Benjamin, Palti the son of Raphu.

10. Of the tribe of Zebulun, Gaddiel the son of Sodi.

11. Of the tribe of Joseph, namely, of the tribe of Manasseh, Gaddi the son of Susi.

12. Of the tribe of Dan, Ammiel the son of Gemalli.

13. Of the tribe of Asher, Sethur the son of Michael.

14. Of the tribe of Naphtali, Nahbi the son of Vophsi.

15. Of the tribe of Gad, Geuel the son of Machi.

16. These are the names of the men that Moses sent to spy out the land. And Moses called Hoshea the son of Nun Joshua.

17. And Moses sent them to spy out the land of Canaan, and said unto them: Get you up here into the South, and go up into the mountains;

18. And see the land, what it is; and the people that dwelleth therein, whether they are strong or weak, whether they are few or many;

19. And what the land is that they dwell in, whether it is good or bad; and what cities they are that they dwell in, whether in camps, or in strongholds;

20. And what the land is, whether it is fat or lean, whether there is wood therein, or not. And be ye of good courage, and bring of the fruit of the land. Now the time was the time of the first-ripe grapes.

21. So, they went up, and spied out the land from the wilderness of Zin unto Rehob, at the entrance to Hamath.

22. And they went up into the South, and came unto Hebron; and Ahiman, Sheshai, and Talmai, the children of Anak, were there. Now Hebron was built seven years before Zoan in Egypt.

23. And they came unto the valley of Eshcol, and cut down from thence a branch with one cluster of grapes, and they bore it upon a pole between two; they took also of the pomegranates, and of the figs.

24. That place was called the valley of Eshcol, because of the cluster which the children of Israel cut down from thence.

25. And they returned from spying out the land at the end of forty days.

26. And they went and came to Moses, and to Aaron, and to all the congregation of the children of Israel, unto the wilderness of Paran, to Kadesh; and brought back word unto them, and unto all the congregation, and showed them the fruit of the land.

27. And they told him, and said: We came unto the land whither thou sentest us, and surely it floweth with milk and honey; and this is the fruit of it.

28. Howbeit the people that dwell in the land are fierce, and the cities are fortified, and very great; and moreover, we saw the children of Anak there.

29. Amalek dwelleth in the land of the South; and the

Hittite, and the Jebusite, and the Amorite, dwell in the mountains; and the Canaanite dwelleth by the sea, and along by the side of the Jordan.

30. And Caleb stilled the people toward Moses, and said: We should go up at once, and possess it; for we are well able to overcome it.

31. But the men that went up with him said: We are not able to go up against the people; for they are stronger than we.

32. And they spread an evil report of the land which they had spied out unto the children of Israel, saying: The land, through which we have passed to spy it out, is a land that eateth up the inhabitants thereof; and all the people that we saw in it are men of great stature.

33. And there we saw the Nephilim, the sons of Anak, who come of the Nephilim; and we were in our own sight as grasshoppers, and so we were in their sight.

Chapter 14

1. And all the congregation lifted up their voice, and cried; and the people wept that night.

2. And all the children of Israel murmured against Moses and against Aaron; and the whole congregation said unto them: Would that we had died in the land of Egypt! or would we had died in this wilderness!

3. And wherefore doth the LORD bring us unto this land, to fall by the sword? Our wives and our little ones will be a prey; were it not better for us to return into Egypt.

4. And they said one to another: Let us make a captain, and let us return into Egypt.

5. Then Moses and Aaron fell on their faces before all the assembly of the congregation of the children of Israel.

6. And Joshua the son of Nun and Caleb the son of Jephunneh, who were of them that spied out the land, rent their clothes.

7. And they spoke unto all the congregation of the children of Israel, saying: The land, which we passed through to spy it out, is an exceeding good land.

8. If the LORD delight in us, then He will bring us into this land, and give it unto us-a land which floweth with milk and honey.

9. Only rebel not against the LORD, neither fear ye the people of the land; for they are bread for us; their defence is removed from over them, and the LORD is with us; fear them not.

10. But all the congregation bade stone them with stones, when the glory of the LORD appeared in the tent of meeting unto all the children of Israel.

11. And the LORD said unto Moses: How long will this people despise Me? and how long will they not believe in Me, for all the signs which I have wrought among them?

12. I will smite them with the pestilence, and destroy them, and will make of thee a nation greater and mightier than they.

13. And Moses said unto the LORD: When the Egyptians shall hear-for Thou broughtest up this people in Thy might from among them.

14. They will say to the inhabitants of this land, who have heard that Thou LORD art in the midst of this people; inasmuch as Thou LORD art seen face to face, and Thy cloud standeth over them, and Thou goest before them, in a pillar of cloud by day, and in a pillar of fire by night;

15. Now if Thou shalt kill this people as one man, then the nations which have heard the fame of Thee will speak, saying:

16. Because the LORD was not able to bring this people into the land which He swore unto them, therefore He hath slain them in the wilderness.

17. And now, I pray Thee, let the power of the Lord be great, according as Thou hast spoken, saying:

18. The LORD is slow to anger, and plenteous in lovingkindness, forgiving iniquity and transgression, and that will by no means clear the guilty; visiting the iniquity of the fathers upon the children, upon the third and upon the fourth generation.

19. Pardon, I pray Thee, the iniquity of this people according unto the greatness of Thy lovingkindness, and according as Thou hast forgiven this people, from Egypt even until now.

20. And the LORD said: I have pardoned according to thy word.

21. But in very deed, as I live-and all the earth shall be filled with the glory of the LORD.

22. Surely all those men that have seen My glory, and My signs, which I wrought in Egypt and in the wilderness, yet have put Me to proof these ten times, and have not hearkened to My voice;

23. Surely, they shall not see the land which I swore unto their fathers, neither shall any of them that despised Me see it.

24. But My servant Caleb, because he had another spirit with him, and hath followed Me fully, him will I bring into the land whereinto he went; and his seed shall possess it.

25. Now the Amalekite and the Canaanite dwell in the Vale; tomorrow turn ye, and get you into the wilderness by the way to the Red Sea.

26. And the LORD spoke unto Moses and unto Aaron, saying:

27. How long shall I bear with this evil congregation, that keep murmuring against Me? I have heard the murmurings of the children of Israel, which they keep murmuring against Me.

28. Say unto them: As I live, saith the LORD, surely as ye have spoken in Mine ears, so will I do to you:

29. Your carcasses shall fall in this wilderness, and all that were numbered of you, according to your whole number, from twenty years old and upward, ye that have murmured against Me;

30. Surely ye shall not come into the land, concerning which I lifted up My hand that I would make you dwell therein, save Caleb the son of Jephunneh, and Joshua the son of Nun.

31. But your little ones, that ye said would be a prey, them will I bring in, and they shall know the land which ye have rejected.

32. But as for you, your carcasses shall fall in this wilderness.

33. And your children shall be wanderers in the wilderness forty years, and shall bear your strayings, until your carcasses be consumed in the wilderness.

34. After the number of the days in which ye spied out the land, even forty days, for every day a year, shall ye bear your iniquities, even forty years, and ye shall know My displeasure.

35. I the LORD have spoken, surely this will I do unto all this evil congregation, that are gathered together against Me; in this wilderness they shall be consumed, and there they shall die.

36. And the men, whom Moses sent to spy out the land, and who, when they returned, made all the congregation to murmur against him, by bringing up an evil report against the land,

37. Even those men that did bring up an evil report of the land, died by the plague before the LORD.

38. But Joshua the son of Nun, and Caleb the son of Jephunneh, remained alive of those men that went to spy out the land.

39. And Moses told these words unto all the children of Israel; and the people mourned greatly.

40. And they rose up early in the morning, and got them up to the top of the mountain, saying: Lo, we are here, and will go up unto the place which the LORD hath promised; for we have sinned.

41. And Moses said: Wherefore now do ye transgress the commandment of the LORD, seeing it shall not prosper?

42. Go not up, for the LORD is not among you; that ye be not smitten down before your enemies.

43. For there the Amalekite and the Canaanite are before you, and ye shall fall by the sword; forasmuch as ye are turned back from following the LORD, and the LORD will not be with you.

44. But they presumed to go up to the top of the mountain; nevertheless, the ark of the covenant of the LORD, and Moses, departed not out of the camp.

45. Then the Amalekite and the Canaanite, who dwelt in that hill-country, came down, and smote them and beat them down, even unto Hormah.

Chapter 15

1. And the LORD spoke unto Moses, saying:

2. Speak unto the children of Israel, and say unto them: When ye are come into the land of your habitations, which I give unto you,

3. And will make an offering by fire unto the LORD, a burnt-offering, or a sacrifice, in fulfilment of a vow clearly uttered, or as a freewill-offering, or in your appointed seasons, to make a sweet savour unto the

LORD, of the herd, or of the flock;

4. Then shall he that bringeth his offering present unto the LORD a meal-offering of a tenth part of an ephah of fine flour mingled with the fourth part of a Hin of oil;

5. And wine for the drink-offering, the fourth part of a Hin, shalt thou prepare with the burnt-offering or for the sacrifice, for each lamb.

6. Or for a ram, thou shalt prepare for a meal-offering two tenth parts of an ephah of fine flour mingled with the third part of a Hin of oil;

7. And for the drink-offering thou shalt present the third part of a Hin of wine, of a sweet savour unto the LORD.

8. And when thou preparest a bullock for a burnt-offering, or for a sacrifice, in fulfilment of a vow clearly uttered, or for peace-offerings unto the LORD;

9. Then shall there be presented with the bullock a meal-offering of three tenth parts of an ephah of fine flour mingled with half a Hin of oil.

10. And thou shalt present for the drink-offering half a Hin of wine, for an offering made by fire, of a sweet savour unto the LORD.

11. Thus, shall it be done for each bullock, or for each ram, or for each of the he-lambs, or of the kids.

12. According to the number that ye may prepare, so shall ye do for every one according to their number.

13. All that are home-born shall do these things after

this manner, in presenting an offering made by fire, of a sweet savour unto the LORD.

14. And if a stranger sojourn with you, or whosoever may be among you, throughout your generations, and will offer an offering made by fire, of a sweet savour unto the LORD; as ye do, so he shall do.

15. As for the congregation, there shall be one statute both for you, and for the stranger that sojourneth with you, a statute for ever throughout your generations; as ye are, so shall the stranger be before the LORD.

16. One law and one ordinance shall be both for you, and for the stranger that sojourneth with you.

17. And the LORD spoke unto Moses, saying:

18. Speak unto the children of Israel, and say unto them: When ye come into the land whither I bring you,

19. Then it shall be, that, when ye eat of the bread of the land, ye shall set apart a portion for a gift unto the LORD.

20. Of the first of your dough ye shall set apart a cake for a gift; as that which is set apart of the threshing-floor, so shall ye set it apart.

21. Of the first of your dough ye shall give unto the LORD a portion for a gift throughout your generations.

22. And when ye shall err, and not observe all these commandments, which the LORD hath spoken unto Moses,

23. Even all that the LORD hath commanded you by

the hand of Moses, from the day that the LORD gave commandment, and onward throughout your generations;

24. Then it shall be, if it be done in error by the congregation, it being hid from their eyes, that all the congregation shall offer one young bullock for a burnt-offering, for a sweet savour unto the LORD-with the meal-offering thereof, and the drink-offering thereof, according to the ordinance-and one he-goat for a sin-offering.

25. And the priest shall make atonement for all the congregation of the children of Israel, and they shall be forgiven; for it was an error, and they have brought their offering, an offering made by fire unto the LORD, and their sin-offering before the LORD, for their error.

26. And all the congregation of the children of Israel shall be forgiven, and the stranger that sojourneth among them; for in respect of all the people it was done in error.

27. And if one person sin through error, then he shall offer a she-goat of the first year for a sin-offering.

28. And the priest shall make atonement for the soul that erreth, when he sinneth through error, before the LORD, to make atonement for him; and he shall be forgiven,

29. Both he that is home-born among the children of Israel, and the stranger that sojourneth among them: ye shall have one law for him that doeth aught in error.

30. But the soul that doeth aught with a high hand, whether he be home-born or a stranger, the same blasphemeth the LORD; and that soul shall be cut off from among his people.

31. Because he hath despised the word of the LORD, and hath broken His commandment; that soul shall utterly be cut off, his iniquity shall be upon him.

32. And while the children of Israel were in the wilderness, they found a man gathering sticks upon the sabbath day.

33. And they that found him gathering sticks brought him unto Moses and Aaron, and unto all the congregation.

34. And they put him in ward, because it had not been declared what should be done to him.

35. And the LORD said unto Moses: The man shall surely be put to death; all the congregation shall stone him with stones without the camp.

36. And all the congregation brought him without the camp, and stoned him with stones, and he died, as the LORD commanded Moses.

37. And the LORD spoke unto Moses, saying:

38. Speak unto the children of Israel, and bid them that they make them throughout their generation's fringes in the corners of their garments, and that they put with the fringe of each corner a thread of blue.

39. And it shall be unto you for a fringe, that ye may look upon it, and remember all the commandments of the LORD, and do them; and that ye go not about after your own heart and your own eyes, after which ye use to go astray;

40. That ye may remember and do all My commandments, and be holy unto your God.

41. I am the LORD your God, who brought you out of the land of Egypt, to be your God: I am the LORD your God.

Korach

Chapter 16

1. Now Korah, the son of Izhar, the son of Kohath, the son of Levi, with Dathan and Abiram, the sons of Eliab, and On, the son of Peleth, sons of Reuben, took men;

2. And they rose up in face of Moses, with certain of the children of Israel, two hundred and fifty men; they were princes of the congregation, the elect men of the assembly, men of renown;

3. And they assembled themselves together against Moses and against Aaron, and said unto them: Ye take too much upon you, seeing all the congregation are holy, every one of them, and the LORD is among them; wherefore then lift ye up yourselves above the assembly of the LORD.

4. And when Moses heard it, he fell upon his face.

5. And he spoke unto Korah and unto all his company, saying: In the morning the LORD will show who are

His, and who is holy, and will cause him to come near unto Him; even him whom He may choose will He cause to come near unto Him.

6. This do - take you censers, Korah, and all his company;

7. And put fire therein, and put incense upon them before the LORD to-morrow; and it shall be that the man whom the LORD doth choose, he shall be holy; ye take too much upon you, ye sons of Levi.

8. And Moses said unto Korah: Hear now, ye sons of Levi:

9. Is it but a small thing unto you, that the God of Israel hath separated you from the congregation of Israel, to bring you near to Himself, to do the service of the tabernacle of the LORD, and to stand before the congregation to minister unto them;

10. And that He hath brought thee near, and all thy brethren the sons of Levi with thee? and will ye seek the priesthood also?

11. Therefore, thou and all thy company that are gathered together against the LORD; and as to Aaron, what is he that ye murmur against him.

12. And Moses sent to call Dathan and Abiram, the sons of Eliab; and they said: We will not come up;

13. Is it a small thing that thou hast brought us up out of a land flowing with milk and honey, to kill us in the wilderness, but thou must needs make thyself also a prince over us?

14. Moreover, thou hast not brought us into a land

flowing with milk and honey, nor given us inheritance of fields and vineyards; wilt thou put out the eyes of these men? we will not come up.

15. And Moses was very wroth, and said unto the LORD: Respect not thou their offering; I have not taken one ass from them, neither have I hurt one of them.

16. And Moses said unto Korah: Be thou and all thy congregation before the LORD, thou, and they, and Aaron, to-morrow;

17. And take ye every man his fire-pan, and put incense upon them, and bring ye before the LORD every man his fire-pan, two hundred and fifty fire-pans; thou also, and Aaron, each his fire-pan.

18. And they took every man his fire-pan, and put fire in them, and laid incense thereon, and stood at the door of the tent of meeting with Moses and Aaron.

19. And Korah assembled all the congregation against them unto the door of the tent of meeting; and the glory of the LORD appeared unto all the congregation.

20. And the LORD spoke unto Moses and unto Aaron, saying:

21. Separate yourselves from among this congregation, that I may consume them in a moment.

22. And they fell upon their faces, and said: O God, the God of the spirits of all flesh, shall one man sin, and wilt Thou be wroth with all the congregation?

23. And the LORD spoke unto Moses, saying:

24. Speak unto the congregation, saying: Get you up from about the dwelling of Korah, Dathan, and Abiram.

25. And Moses rose up and went unto Dathan and Abiram; and the elders of Israel followed him.

26. And he spoke unto the congregation, saying: Depart, I pray you, from the tents of these wicked men, and touch nothing of theirs, lest ye be swept away in all their sins.

27. So, they got them up from the dwelling of Korah, Dathan, and Abiram, on every side; and Dathan and Abiram came out, and stood at the door of their tents, with their wives, and their sons, and their little ones.

28. And Moses said: Hereby ye shall know that the LORD hath sent me to do all these works, and that I have not done them of mine own mind.

29. If these men die the common death of all men, and be visited after the visitation of all men, then the LORD hath not sent Me.

30. But if the LORD make a new thing, and the ground open her mouth, and swallow them up, with all that appertain unto them, and they go down alive into the pit, then ye shall understand that these men have despised the LORD.

31. And it came to pass, as he made an end of speaking all these words, that the ground did cleave asunder that was under them.

32. And the earth opened her mouth and swallowed them up, and their households, and all the men that appertained unto Korah, and all their goods.

33. So, they, and all that appertained to them, went down alive into the pit; and the earth closed upon them, and they perished from among the assembly.

34. And all Israel that were round about them fled at the cry of them; for they said: Lest the earth swallow us up.

35. And fire came forth from the LORD, and devoured the two hundred and fifty men that offered the incense.

Chapter 17

1. And the LORD spoke unto Moses, saying:

2. Speak unto Eleazar the son of Aaron the priest, that he take up the fire-pans out of the burning, and scatter thou the fire yonder; for they are become holy;

3. Even the fire-pans of these men who have sinned at the cost of their lives, and let them be made beaten plates for a covering of the altar-for they are become holy, because they were offered before the LORD-that they may be a sign unto the children of Israel.

4. And Eleazar the priest took the brazen fire-pans, which thcy that were burnt had offered; and they beat them out for a covering of the altar,

5. To be a memorial unto the children of Israel, to the end that no common man, that is not of the seed of Aaron, draw near to burn incense before the LORD; that he fare not as Korah, and as his company; as the LORD spoke unto him by the hand of Moses.

6. But on the morrow, all the congregation of the children of Israel murmured against Moses and against Aaron, saying: Ye have killed the people of the LORD.

7. And it came to pass, when the congregation was assembled against Moses and against Aaron, that they looked toward the tent of meeting; and, behold, the cloud covered it, and the glory of the LORD appeared.

8. And Moses and Aaron came to the front of the tent of meeting.

9. And the LORD spoke unto Moses, saying:

10. Get you up from among this congregation, that I may consume them in a moment. And they fell upon their faces.

11. And Moses said unto Aaron: Take thy fire-pan, and put fire therein from off the altar, and lay incense thereon, and carry it quickly unto the congregation, and make atonement for them; for there is wrath gone out from the LORD: the plague is begun.

12. And Aaron took as Moses spoke, and ran into the midst of the assembly; and, behold, the plague was begun among the people; and he put on the incense, and made atonement for the people.

13. And he stood between the dead and the living; and the plague was stayed.

14. Now they that died by the plague were fourteen thousand and seven hundred, besides them that died about the matter of Korah.

15. And Aaron returned unto Moses unto the door of the tent of meeting, and the plague was stayed.

16. And the LORD spoke unto Moses, saying:

17. Speak unto the children of Israel, and take of them rods, one for each fathers' house, of all their princes according to their fathers' houses, twelve rods; thou shalt write every man's name upon his rod.

18. And thou shalt write Aaron's name upon the rod of Levi, for there shall be one rod for the head of their fathers' houses.

19. And thou shalt lay them up in the tent of meeting before the testimony, where I meet with you.

20. And it shall come to pass, that the man whom I shall choose, his rod shall bud; and I will make to cease from Me the murmurings of the children of Israel, which they murmur against you.

21. And Moses spoke unto the children of Israel; and all their princes gave him rods, for each prince one, according to their fathers' houses, even twelve rods; and the rod of Aaron was among their rods.

22. And Moses laid up the rods before the LORD in the tent of the testimony.

23. And it came to pass on the morrow, that Moses went into the tent of the testimony; and, behold, the rod of Aaron for the house of Levi was budded, and put forth buds, and bloomed blossoms, and bore ripe almonds.

24. And Moses brought out all the rods from before the LORD unto all the children of Israel; and they looked, and took every man his rod.

25. And the LORD said unto Moses: Put back the rod of Aaron before the testimony, to be kept there, for a token against the rebellious children; that there may be made an end of their murmurings against Me, that they die not.

26. Thus did Moses; as the LORD commanded him, so did he.

27. And the children of Israel spoke unto Moses, saying: **Behold** we perish, we are undone, we are all undone.

28. Every one that cometh near, that cometh near unto the tabernacle of the LORD, is to die; shall we wholly perish.

Chapter 18

1. And the LORD said unto Aaron: Thou and thy sons and thy fathers' house with thee shall bear the iniquity of the sanctuary; and thou and thy sons with thee shall bear the iniquity of your priesthood.

2. And thy brethren also, the tribe of Levi, the tribe of thy father, bring thou near with thee, that they may be joined unto thee, and minister unto thee, thou and thy sons with thee being before the tent of the testimony.

3. And they shall keep thy charge, and the charge of all the Tent; only they shall not come nigh unto the holy furniture and unto the altar, that they die not, neither they, nor ye.

4. And they shall be joined unto thee, and keep the

charge of the tent of meeting, whatsoever the service of the Tent may be; but a common man shall not draw nigh unto you.

5. And ye shall keep the charge of the holy things, and the charge of the altar, that there be wrath no more upon the children of Israel.

6. And I, behold, I have taken your brethren the Levites from among the children of Israel; for you they are given as a gift unto the LORD, to do the service of the tent of meeting.

7. And thou and thy sons with thee shall keep your priesthood in everything that pertaineth to the altar, and to that within the veil; and ye shall serve; I give you the priesthood as a service of gift; and the common man that draweth nigh shall be put to death.

8. And the LORD spoke unto Aaron: And I, behold, I have given thee the charge of My heave-offerings; even of all the hallowed things of the children of Israel unto thee have I given them for a consecrated portion, and to thy sons, as a due for ever.

9. This shall be thine of the most holy things, reserved from the fire: every offering of theirs, even every meal-offering of theirs, and every sin-offering of theirs, and every guilt-offering of theirs, which they may render unto Me, shall be most holy for thee and for thy sons.

10. In a most holy place shalt thou eat thereof; every male may eat thereof; it shall be holy unto thee.

11. And this is thine: the heave-offering of their gift, even all the wave-offerings of the children of Israel; I have given them unto thee, and to thy sons and to thy daughters with thee, as a due for ever; every one that is clean in thy house may eat thereof.

12. All the best of the oil, and all the best of the wine, and of the corn, the first part of them which they give unto the LORD, to thee have I given them.

13. The first-ripe fruits of all that is in their land, which they bring unto the LORD, shall be thine; every one that is clean in thy house may eat thereof.

14. Every thing devoted in Israel shall be thine.

15. Every thing that opened the womb, of all flesh which they offer unto the LORD, both of man and beast, shall be thine; howbeit the first-born of man shalt thou surely redeem, and the firstling of unclean beasts shalt thou redeem.

16. And their redemption-money-from a month old shalt thou redeem them-shall be, according to thy valuation, five shekels of silver, after the shekel of the sanctuary-the same is twenty gerahs.

17. But the firstling of an ox, or the firstling of a sheep, or the firstling of a goat, thou shalt not redeem; they are holy: thou shalt dash their blood against the altar, and shalt make their fat smoke for an offering made by fire, for a sweet savour unto the LORD.

18. And the flesh of them shall be thine, as the wave-breast and as the right thigh, it shall be thine.

19. All the heave-offerings of the holy things, which the children of Israel offer unto the LORD, have I given thee, and thy sons and thy daughters with thee, as a due for ever; it is an everlasting covenant of salt before the LORD unto thee and to thy seed with thee.

20. And the LORD said unto Aaron: Thou shalt have no inheritance in their land, neither shalt thou have any portion among them; I am thy portion and thine inheritance among the children of Israel.

21. And unto the children of Levi, behold, I have given all the tithe in Israel for an inheritance, in return for their service which they serve, even the service of the tent of meeting.

22. And henceforth the children of Israel shall not come nigh the tent of meeting, lest they bear sin, and die.

23. But the Levites alone shall do the service of the tent of meeting, and they shall bear their iniquity; it shall be a statute for ever throughout your generations, and among the children of Israel they shall have no inheritance.

24. For the tithe of the children of Israel, which they set apart as a gift unto the LORD, I have given to the Levites for an inheritance; therefore, I have said unto them: Among the children of Israel, they shall have no inheritance.

25. And the LORD spoke unto Moses, saying:

26. Moreover, thou shalt speak unto the Levites, and say unto them: When ye take of the children of Israel the tithe which I have given you from them for your inheritance, then ye shall set apart of it a gift for the

LORD, even a tithe of the tithe.

27. And the gift which ye set apart shall be reckoned unto you, as though it were the corn of the threshing-floor, and as the fulness of the wine-press.

28. Thus, ye also shall set apart a gift unto the LORD of all your tithes, which ye receive of the children of Israel; and thereof ye shall give the gift which is set apart unto the LORD to Aaron the priest.

29. Out of all that is given you ye shall set apart all of that which is due unto the LORD, of all the best thereof, even the hallowed part thereof out of it.

30. Therefore, thou shalt say unto them: When ye set apart the best thereof from it, then it shall be counted unto the Levites as the increase of the threshing-floor, and as the increase of the wine-press.

31. And ye may eat it in every place, ye and your households; for it is your reward in return for your service in the tent of meeting.

32. And ye shall bear no sin by reason of it, seeing that ye have set apart from it the best thereof; and ye shall not profane the holy things of the children of Israel, that ye die not.

Chukat

Chapter 19

1. And the LORD spoke unto Moses and unto Aaron, saying:

2. This is the statute of the law which the LORD hath

commanded, saying: Speak unto the children of Israel, that they bring thee a red heifer, faultless, wherein is no blemish, and upon which never came yoke.

3. And ye shall give her unto Eleazar the priest, and she shall be brought forth without the camp, and she shall be slain before his face.

4. And Eleazar the priest shall take of her blood with his finger, and sprinkle of her blood toward the front of the tent of meeting seven times.

5. And the heifer shall be burnt in his sight; her skin, and her flesh, and her blood, with her dung, shall be burnt.

6. And the priest shall take cedar-wood, and hyssop, and scarlet, and cast it into the midst of the burning of the heifer.

7. Then the priest shall wash his clothes, and he shall bathe his flesh in water, and afterward he may come into the camp, and the priest shall be unclean until the even.

8. And he that burneth her shall wash his clothes in water, and bathe his flesh in water, and shall be unclean until the even.

9. And a man that is clean shall gather up the ashes of the heifer, and lay them up without the camp in a clean place, and it shall be kept for the congregation of the children of Israel for a water of sprinkling; it is a purification from sin.

10. And he that gathereth the ashes of the heifer shall

wash his clothes, and be unclean until the even; and it shall be unto the children of Israel, and unto the stranger that sojourneth among them, for a statute for ever.

11. He that toucheth the dead, even any man's dead body, shall be unclean seven days;

12. The same shall purify himself therewith on the third day and on the seventh day, and he shall be clean; but if he purify not himself the third day and the seventh day, he shall not be clean.

13. Whosoever toucheth the dead, even the body of any man that is dead, and purifieth not himself-he hath defiled the tabernacle of the LORD-that soul shall be cut off from Israel; because the water of sprinkling was not dashed against him, he shall be unclean; his uncleanness is yet upon him.

14. This is the law: when a man dieth in a tent, every one that cometh into the tent, and every thing that is in the tent, shall be unclean seven days.

15. And every open vessel, which hath no covering close-bound upon it, is unclean.

16. And whosoever in the open field toucheth one that is slain with a sword, or one that dieth of himself, or a bone of a man, or a grave, shall be unclean seven days.

17. And for the unclean they shall take of the ashes of the burning of the purification from sin, and running water shall be put thereto in a vessel.

18. And a clean person shall take hyssop, and dip it in

the water, and sprinkle it upon the tent, and upon all the vessels, and upon the persons that were there, and upon him that touched the bone, or the slain, or the dead, or the grave.

19. And the clean person shall sprinkle upon the unclean on the third day, and on the seventh day; and on the seventh day he shall purify him; and he shall wash his clothes, and bathe himself in water, and shall be clean at even.

20. But the man that shall be unclean, and shall not purify himself, that soul shall be cut off from the midst of the assembly, because he hath defiled the sanctuary of the LORD; the water of sprinkling hath not been dashed against him: he is unclean.

21. And it shall be a perpetual statute unto them; and he that sprinkleth the water of sprinkling shall wash his clothes; and he that toucheth the water of sprinkling shall be unclean until even.

22. And whatsoever the unclean person toucheth shall be unclean; and the soul that toucheth him shall be unclean until even.

Chapter 20

1. And the children of Israel, even the whole congregation, came into the wilderness of Zin in the first month; and the people abode in Kadesh; and Miriam died there, and was buried there.

2. And there was no water for the congregation; and they assembled themselves together against Moses and against Aaron.

3. And the people strove with Moses, and spoke, saying: Would that we had perished when our brethren perished before the LORD!

4. And why have ye brought the assembly of the LORD into this wilderness, to die there, we and our cattle?

5. And wherefore have ye made us to come up out of Egypt, to bring us in unto this evil place? it is no place of seed, or of figs, or of vines, or of pomegranates; neither is there any water to drink.

6. And Moses and Aaron went from the presence of the assembly unto the door of the tent of meeting, and fell upon their faces; and the glory of the LORD appeared unto them.

7. And the LORD spoke unto Moses, saying:

8. Take the rod, and assemble the congregation, thou, and Aaron thy brother, and speak ye unto the rock before their eyes, that it give forth its water; and thou shalt bring forth to them water out of the rock; so thou shalt give the congregation and their cattle drink.

9. And Moses took the rod from before the LORD, as He commanded him.

10. And Moses and Aaron gathered the assembly together before the rock, and he said unto them: Hear now, ye rebels; are we to bring you forth water out of this rock.

11. And Moses lifted up his hand, and smote the rock with his rod twice; and water came forth abundantly, and the congregation drank, and their cattle.

12. And the LORD said unto Moses and Aaron: Because ye believed not in Me, to sanctify Me in the eyes of the children of Israel, therefore ye shall not bring this assembly into the land which I have given them.

13. These are the waters of Meribah, where the children of Israel strove with the LORD, and He was sanctified in them.

14. And Moses sent messengers from Kadesh unto the king of Edom: Thus, saith thy brother Israel: Thou knowest all the travail that hath befallen us;

15. How our fathers went down into Egypt, and we dwelt in Egypt a long time; and the Egyptians dealt ill with us, and our fathers;

16. And when we cried unto the LORD, He heard our voice, and sent an angel, and brought us forth out of Egypt; and, behold, we are in Kadesh, a city in the uttermost of thy border.

17. Let us pass, I pray thee, through thy land; we will not pass through field or through vineyard, neither will we drink of the water of the wells; we will go along the king's highway, we will not turn aside to the right hand nor to the left, until we have passed thy border.

18. And Edom said unto him: Thou shalt not pass through me, lest I come out with the sword against thee.

19. And the children of Israel said unto him: We will

go up by the highway; and if we drink of thy water, I and my cattle, then will I give the price thereof; let me only pass through on my feet; there is no hurt.

20. And he said: Thou shalt not pass through. And Edom came out against him with much people, and with a strong hand.

21. Thus, Edom refused to give Israel passage through his border; wherefore Israel turned away from him.

22. And they journeyed from Kadesh; and the children of Israel, even the whole congregation, came unto mount Hor.

23. And the LORD spoke unto Moses and Aaron in mount **Hor**, by the border of the land of Edom, saying:

24. Aaron shall be gathered unto his people; for he shall not enter into the land which I have given unto the children of Israel, because ye rebelled against My word at the waters of Meribah.

25. Take Aaron and Eleazar his son, and bring them up unto mount Hor.

26. And strip Aaron of his garments, and put them upon Eleazar his son; and Aaron shall be gathered unto his people, and shall die there.

27. And Moses did as the LORD commanded; and they went up into mount Hor in the sight of all the congregation.

28. And Moses stripped Aaron of his garments, and put them upon Eleazar his son; and Aaron died there in the top of the mount; and Moses and Eleazar came down from the mount.

29. And when all the congregation saw that Aaron was dead, they wept for Aaron thirty days, even all the house of Israel.

Chapter 21

1. And the Canaanite, the king of Arad, who dwelt in the South, heard tell that Israel came by the way of Atharim; and he fought against Israel, and took some of them captive.

2. And Israel vowed a vow unto the LORD, and said: If Thou wilt indeed deliver this people into my hand, then I will utterly destroy their cities.

3. And the LORD hearkened to the voice of Israel, and delivered up the Canaanites; and they utterly destroyed them and their cities; and the name of the place was called Hormah.

4. And they journeyed from mount Hor by the way to the Red Sea, to compass the land of Edom; and the soul of the people became impatient because of the way.

5. And the people spoke against God, and against Moses: Wherefore have ye brought us up out of Egypt to die in the wilderness? for there is no bread, and there is no water; and our soul loatheth this light bread.

6. And the LORD sent fiery serpents among the people, and they bit the people; and much people of

Israel died.

7. And the people came to Moses, and said: We have sinned, because we have spoken against the LORD, and against thee; pray unto the LORD, that He take away the serpents from us. And Moses prayed for the people.

8. And the LORD said unto Moses: Make thee a fiery serpent, and set it upon a pole; and it shall come to pass, that every one that is bitten, when he seeth it, shall live.

9. And Moses made a serpent of brass, and set it upon the pole; and it came to pass, that if a serpent had bitten any man, when he looked unto the serpent of brass, he lived.

10. And the children of Israel journeyed, and pitched in Oboth.

11. And they journeyed from Oboth, and pitched at Ije-abarim, in the wilderness which is in front of Moab, toward the sun-rising.

12. From thence they journeyed, and pitched in the valley of Zered.

13. From thence they journeyed, and pitched on the other side of the Arnon, which is in the wilderness, that cometh out of the border of the Amorites. For Arnon is the border of Moab, between Moab and the Amorites;

14. Wherefore it is said in the book of the Wars of the LORD: Vaheb in Suphah, And the valleys of Arnon,

15. And the slope of the valleys That inclineth toward

the seat of Ar, And leaneth upon the border of Moab.

16. And from thence to Beer; that is the well whereof the LORD said unto Moses: Gather the people together, and I will give them water.

17. Then sang Israel this song: Spring up, O well-sing ye unto it.

18. The well, which the princes digged, Which the nobles of the people delved, With the sceptre, and with their staves. And from the wilderness to Mattanah;

19. And from Mattanah to Nahaliel; and from Nahaliel to Bamoth;

20. And from Bamoth to the valley that is in the field of Moab, by the top of Pisgah, which looketh down upon the desert.

21. And Israel sent messengers unto Sihon king of the Amorites, saying:

22. Let me pass through thy land; we will not turn aside into field, or into vineyard; we will not drink of the water of the wells; we will go by the king's highway, until we have passed thy border.

23. And Sihon would not suffer Israel to pass through his border; but Sihon gathered all his people together, and went out against Israel into the wilderness, and came to Jahaz; and he fought against Israel.

24. And Israel smote him with the edge of the sword, and possessed his land from the Arnon unto the Jabbok, even unto the children of Ammon; for the border of the children of Ammon was strong.

25. And Israel took all these cities; and Israel dwelt in all the cities of the Amorites, in Heshbon, and in all the towns thereof.

26. For Heshbon was the city of Sihon the king of the Amorites, who had fought against the former king of Moab, and taken all his land out of his hand, even unto the Arnon.

27. Wherefore they that speak in parables say: Come ye to Heshbon! Let the city of Sihon be built and established!

28. For a fire is gone out of Heshbon, A flame from the city of Sihon; It hath devoured Ar of Moab, The lords of the high places of Arnon.

29. Woe to thee, Moab! Thou art undone, O people of Chemosh; He hath given his sons as fugitives, And his daughters into captivity, Unto Sihon king of the Amorites.

30. We have shot at them-Heshbon is perished-even unto Dibon. And we have laid waste even unto Nophah, Which reacheth unto Medeba.

31. Thus, Israel dwelt in the land of the Amorites.

32. And Moses sent to spy out Jazer, and they took the towns thereof, and drove out the Amorites that were there.

33. And they turned and went up by the way of Bashan; and Og the king of Bashan went out against them, he and all his people, to battle at Edrei.

34. And the LORD said unto Moses: Fear him not; for I have delivered him into thy hand, and all his people, and his land; and thou shalt do to him as thou didst unto Sihon king of the Amorites, who dwelt at Heshbon.

35. So, they smote him, and his sons, and all his people, until there was none left him remaining; and they possessed his land.

Chapter 22

1. And the children of Israel journeyed, and pitched in the plains of Moab beyond the Jordan at Jericho.

Balak

2. And Balak the son of Zippor saw all that Israel had done to the Amorites.

3. And Moab was sore afraid of the people, because they were many; and Moab was overcome with dread because of the children of Israel.

4. And Moab said unto the elders of Midian: Now will this multitude lick up all that is round about us, as the ox licketh up the grass of the field. And Balak the son of Zippor was king of Moab at that time.

5. And he sent messengers unto Balaam the son of Beor, to Pethor, which is by the River, to the land of the children of his people, to call him, saying: Behold, there is a people come out from Egypt; behold, they cover the face of the earth, and they abide over against me.

6. Come now therefore, I pray thee, curse me this

people; for they are too mighty for me; peradventure I shall prevail, that we may smite them, and that I may drive them out of the land; for I know that he whom thou blessest is blessed, and he whom thou cursest is cursed.

7. And the elders of Moab and the elders of Midian departed with the rewards of divination in their hand; and they came unto Balaam, and spoke unto him the words of Balak.

8. And he said unto them: Lodge here this night, and I will bring you back word, as the LORD may speak unto me; and the princes of Moab abode with Balaam.

9. And God came unto Balaam, and said: What men are these with thee.

10. And Balaam said unto God: Balak the son of Zippor, king of Moab, hath sent unto me saying:

11. Behold the people that is come out of Egypt, it covereth the face of the earth; now, come curse me them; peradventure I shall be able to fight against them, and shall drive them out.

12. And God said unto Balaam: Thou shalt not go with them; thou shalt not curse the people; for they are blessed.

13. And Balaam rose up in the morning, and said unto the princes of Balak: Get you into your land; for the LORD refuseth to give me leave to go with you.

14. And the princes of Moab rose up, and they went unto Balak, and said: Balaam refuseth to come with us.

15. And Balak sent yet again princes, more, and more honourable than they.

16. And they came to Balaam, and said to him: Thus saith Balak the son of Zippor: Let nothing, I pray thee - Hinder thee from coming unto me;

17. For I will promote thee unto very great honour, and whatsoever thou sayest unto me I will do; come therefore, I pray thee, curse me this people.

18. And Balaam answered and said unto the servants of Balak: If Balak would give me his house full of silver and gold, I cannot go beyond the word of the LORD my God, to do any thing, small or great.

19. Now therefore, I pray you, tarry ye also here this night, that I may know what the LORD will speak unto me more.

20. And God came unto Balaam at night, and said unto him: If the men are come to call thee, rise up, go with them; but only the word which I speak unto thee, that shalt thou do.

21. And Balaam rose up in the morning, and saddled his ass, and went with the princes of Moab.

22. And God's anger was kindled because he went; and the angel of the LORD placed himself in the way for an adversary against him. Now he was riding upon his ass, and his two servants were with him.

23. And the ass saw the angel of the LORD standing in the way, with his sword drawn in his hand; and the ass turned aside out of the way, and went into the field; and Balaam smote the ass, to turn her into the way.

24. Then the angel of the LORD stood in a hollow way between the vineyards, a fence being on this side, and a fence on that side.

25. And the ass saw the angel of the LORD, and she thrust herself unto the wall, and crushed Balaam's foot against the wall; and he smote her again.

26. And the angel of the LORD went further, and stood in a narrow place, where was no way to turn either to the right hand or to the left.

27. And the ass saw the angel of the LORD, and she lay down under Balaam; and Balaam's anger was kindled, and he smote the ass with his staff.

28. And the LORD opened the mouth of the ass, and she said unto Balaam: What have I done unto thee, that thou hast smitten me these three times.

29. And Balaam said unto the ass: Because thou hast mocked me; I would there were a sword in my hand, for now I had killed thee.

30. And the ass said unto Balaam: Am not I thine ass, upon which thou hast ridden all thy life long unto this day? was I ever wont to do so unto thee. And he said: Nay.

31. Then the LORD opened the eyes of Balaam, and he saw the angel of the LORD standing in the way, with his sword drawn in his hand; and he bowed his head, and fell on his face.

32. And the angel of the LORD said unto him: Wherefore hast thou smitten thine ass these three times? behold, I am come forth for an adversary, because thy way is contrary unto me;

33. And the ass saw me, and turned aside before me these three times; unless she had turned aside from me, surely now I had even slain thee, and saved her alive.

34. And Balaam said unto the angel of the LORD: I have sinned; for I knew not that thou stoodest in the way against me; now therefore, if it displease thee, I will get me back.

35. And the angel of the LORD said unto Balaam: Go with the men; but only the word that I shall speak unto thee, that thou shalt speak. So, Balaam went with the princes of Balak.

36. And when Balak heard that Balaam was come, he went out to meet him unto Ir-moab, which is on the border of Arnon, which is in the utmost part of the border.

37. And Balak said unto Balaam: Did I not earnestly send unto thee to call thee? wherefore camest thou not unto me? am I not able indeed to promote thee to honour.

38. And Balaam said unto Balak: Lo, I am come unto thee; have I now any power at all to speak any thing? the word that God putteth in my mouth, that shall I speak.

39. And Balaam went with Balak, and they came unto Kiriath-huzoth.

40. And Balak sacrificed oxen and sheep, and sent to

Balaam, and to the princes that were with him.

41. And it came to pass in the morning that Balak took Balaam, and brought him up into Bamoth-baal, and he saw from thence the utmost part of the people.

Chapter 23

1. And Balaam said unto Balak: Build me here seven altars, and prepare me here seven bullocks and seven rams.

2. And Balak did as Balaam had spoken; and Balak and Balaam offered on every altar a bullock and a ram.

3. And Balaam said unto Balak: Stand by thy burnt-offering, and I will go; peradventure the LORD will come to meet me; and whatsoever He showeth me I will tell thee. And he went to a bare height.

4. And God met Balaam; and he said unto Him: I have prepared the seven altars, and I have offered up a bullock and a ram on every altar.

5. And the LORD put a word in Balaam's mouth, and said: Return unto Balak, and thus thou shalt speak.

6. And he returned unto him, and, lo, he stood by his burnt-offering, he, and all the princes of Moab.

7. And he took up his parable, and said: From Aram Balak bringeth me. The king of Moab from the mountains of the East: Come, curse me Jacob, and come, execrate Israel.

8. How shall I curse, whom God hath not cursed? And how shall I execrate, whom the LORD hath not

Execrated.

9. For from the top of the rocks I see him, and from the hills I behold him: Lo, it is a people that shall dwell alone, and shall not be reckoned among the nations.

10. Who hath counted the dust of Jacob, or numbered the stock of Israel? Let me die the death of the righteous, and let mine end be like his!

11. And Balak said unto Balaam: What hast thou done unto me? I took thee to curse mine enemies, and, behold, thou hast blessed them altogether.

12. And he answered and said: Must I not take heed to speak that which the LORD putteth in my mouth.

13. And Balak said unto him: Come, I pray thee, with me unto another place, from whence thou mayest see them; thou shalt see but the utmost part of them, and shalt not see them all; and curse me them from thence.

14. And he took him into the field of Zophim, to the top of Pisgah, and built seven altars, and offered up a bullock and a ram on every altar.

15. And he said unto Balak: Stand here by thy burnt-offering, while I go toward a meeting yonder.

16. And the LORD met Balaam, and put a word in his mouth, and said: Return unto Balak, and thus shalt thou speak.

17. And he came to him, and, lo, he stood by his burnt-offering, and the princes of Moab with him. And Balak said unto him: What hath the LORD spoken.

18. And he took up his parable, and said: Arise, Balak, and hear; Give ear unto me, thou son of Zippor:

19. God is not a man, that He should lie; Neither the son of man, that He should repent: When He hath said, will He not do it? Or when He hath spoken, will He not make it good?

20. Behold, I am bidden to bless; And when He hath blessed, I cannot call it back.

21. None hath beheld iniquity in Jacob, neither hath one seen perverseness in Israel; The LORD his God is with him, And the shouting for the King is among them.

22. God who brought them forth out of Egypt Is for them like the lofty horns of the wild-ox.

23. For there is no enchantment with Jacob, neither is there any divination with Israel; Now is it said of Jacob and of Israel: What hath God wrought!

24. Behold a people that riseth up as a lioness. And as a lion doth he lift himself up; He shall not lie down until he eat of the prey, And drink the blood of the slain.

25. And Balak said unto Balaam: Neither curse them at all, nor bless them at all

26. But Balaam answered and said unto Balak: Told not I thee, saying: All that the LORD speaketh, that I must do.

27. And Balak said unto Balaam: Come now, I will take thee unto another place; peradventure it will please God that thou mayest curse me them from thence.

28. And Balak took Balaam unto the top of Peor, that looketh down upon the desert.

29. And Balaam said unto Balak: Build me here seven altars, and prepare me here seven bullocks and seven rams.

30. And Balak did as Balaam had said, and offered up a bullock and a ram on every altar.

Chapter 24

1. And when Balaam saw that it pleased the LORD to bless Israel, he went not, as at the other times, to meet with enchantments, but he set his face toward the wilderness.

2. And Balaam lifted up his eyes, and he saw Israel dwelling tribe by tribe; and the spirit of God came upon him.

3. And he took up his parable, and said: The saying of Balaam the son of Beor, And the saying of the man whose eye is opened;

4. The saying of him who heareth the words of God, who seeth the vision of the Almighty, Fallen down, yet with opened eyes:

5. How goodly are thy tents, O Jacob, Thy dwellings, O Israel!

6. As valleys stretched out, as gardens by the river-side; As aloes planted of the LORD, As cedars beside the waters;

7. Water shall flow from his branches, and his seed shall be in many waters; And his king shall be higher than Agag, and his kingdom shall be exalted.

8. God who brought him forth out of Egypt Is for him like the lofty horns of the wild-ox; He shall eat up the nations that are his adversaries, and shall break their bones in pieces, and pierce them through with his arrows.

9. He couched, he lay down as a lion, and as a lioness; who shall rouse him up? Blessed be every one that blesseth thee, and cursed be every one that curseth thee.

10. And Balak's anger was kindled against Balaam, and he smote his hands together; and Balak said unto Balaam: I called thee to curse mine enemies, and, behold, thou hast altogether blessed them these three times.

11. Therefore, now flee thou to thy place; I thought to promote thee unto great honour; but, lo, the LORD hath kept thee back from honour.

12. And Balaam said unto Balak: Spoke I not also to thy messengers that thou didst send unto me, saying:

13. If Balak would give me his house full of silver and gold, I cannot go beyond the word of the LORD, to do either good or bad of mine own mind; what the LORD speaketh, that will I speak?

14. And now, behold, I go unto my people; come, and I will announce to thee what this people shall do to thy people in the end of days.

15. And he took up his parable, and said: The saying of Balaam the son of Beor, And the saying of the man whose eye is opened;

16. The saying of him who heareth the words of God, and knoweth the knowledge of the Most High, Who seeth the vision of the Almighty, Fallen down, yet with opened eyes:

17. I see him, but not now; I behold him, but not nigh; There shall step forth a star out of Jacob, and a scepter shall rise out of Israel; And shall smite through the corners of Moab; And break down all the sons of Seth.

18. And Edom shall be a possession, Seir also, even his enemies, shall be a possession; While Israel doeth valiantly.

19. And out of Jacob shall one have dominion, and shall destroy the remnant from the city.

20. And he looked on Amalek, and took up his parable, and said: Amalek was the first of the nations; But his end shall come to destruction.

21. And he looked on the Kenite, and took up his parable, and said: Though firm be thy dwelling-place, and though thy nest be set in the rock;

22. Nevertheless, Kain shall be wasted; How long? Asshur shall carry thee away captive.

23. And he took up his parable, and said: Alas, who shall live after God hath appointed him?

24. But ships shall come from the coast of Kittim, and they shall afflict Asshur, and shall afflict Eber, and he also, shall come to destruction.

25. And Balaam rose up, and went and returned to his place; and Balak also went his way.

Chapter 25

1. And Israel abode in Shittim, and the people began to commit harlotry with the daughters of Moab.

2. And they called the people unto the sacrifices of their gods; and the people did eat, and bowed down to their gods.

3. And Israel joined himself unto the Baal of Peor; and the anger of the LORD was kindled against Israel.

4. And the LORD said unto Moses: Take all the chiefs of the people, and hang them up unto the LORD in face of the sun, that the fierce anger of the LORD may turn away from Israel.

5. And Moses said unto the judges of Israel: Slay ye every one his men that have joined themselves unto the Baal of Peor.

6. And, behold, one of the children of Israel came and brought unto his brethren a Midianitish woman in the sight of Moses, and in the sight of all the congregation of the children of Israel, while they were weeping at the door of the tent of meeting.

7. And when Phinehas, the son of Eleazar, the son of Aaron the priest, saw it, he rose up from the midst of the congregation, and took a spear in his hand.

8. And he went after the man of Israel into the chamber, and thrust both of them through, the man of

Israel, and the woman through her belly. So, the plague was stayed from the children of Israel.

9. And those that died by the plague were twenty and four thousand.

Pinchas

10. And the LORD spoke unto Moses, saying:

11. Phinehas, the son of Eleazar, the son of Aaron the priest, hath turned My wrath away from the children of Israel, in that he was very jealous for My sake among them, so that I consumed not the children of Israel in My jealousy.

12. Wherefore say: Behold, I give unto him My covenant of peace;

13. And it shall be unto him, and to his seed after him, the covenant of an everlasting priesthood; because he was jealous for his God, and made atonement for the children of Israel.

14. Now the name of the man of Israel that was slain, who was slain with the Midianitish woman, was Zimri, the son of Salu, a prince of a fathers' house among thc Simeonites.

15. And the name of the Midianitish woman that was slain was Cozbi, the daughter of Zur; he was head of the people of a fathers' house in Midian.

16. And the LORD spoke unto Moses, saying:

17. Harass the Midianites, and smite them;

18. For they harass you, by their wiles wherewith they

have beguiled you in the matter of Peor, and in the matter of Cozbi, the daughter of the prince of Midian, their sister, who was slain on the day of the plague in the matter of Peor.

Chapter 26

1. And it came to pass after the plague, that the LORD spoke unto Moses and unto Eleazar the son of Aaron the priest, saying:

2. Take the sum of all the congregation of the children of Israel, from twenty years old and upward, by their fathers' houses, all that are able to go forth to war in Israel.

3. And Moses and Eleazar the priest spoke with them in the plains of Moab by the Jordan at Jericho, saying:

4. Take the sum of the people, from twenty years old and upward, as the LORD commanded Moses and the children of Israel, that came forth out of the land of Egypt.

5. Reuben, the first-born of Israel: the sons of Reuben: of Hanoch, the family of the Hanochites; of Pallu, the family of the Palluites;

6. Of Hezron, the family of the Hezronites; of Carmi, the family of the Carmites.

7. These are the families of the Reubenites; and they that were numbered of them were forty and three thousand and seven hundred and thirty.

8. And the sons of Pallu: Eliab.

9. And the sons of Eliab: Nemuel, and Dathan, and

Abiram. These are that Dathan and Abiram, the elect of the congregation, who strove against Moses and against Aaron in the company of Korah, when they strove against the LORD;

10. And the earth opened her mouth, and swallowed them up together with Korah, when that company died; what time the fire devoured two hundred and fifty men, and they became a sign.

11. Notwithstanding the sons of Korah died not.

12. The sons of Simeon after their families: of Nemuel, the family of the Nemuelites; of Jamin, the family of the Jaminites; of JacHin, the family of the JacHinites;

13. Of Zerah, the family of the Zerahites; of Shaul, the family of the Shaulites.

14. These are the families of the Simeonites, twenty and two thousand and two hundred.

15. The sons of Gad after their families: of Zephon, the family of the Zephonites; of Haggi, the family of the Haggites; of Shuni, the family of the Shunites;

16. Of Ozni, the family of the Oznites; of Eri, the family of the Erites;

17. Of Arod, the family of the Arodites; of Areli, the family of the Arelites.

18. These are the families of the sons of Gad according to those that were numbered of them, forty thousand and five hundred.

19. The sons of Judah: Er and Onan; and Er and Onan died in the land of Canaan.

20. And the sons of Judah after their families were: of Shelah, the family of the Shelanites; of Perez, the family of the Perezites; of Zerah, the family of the Zerahites.

21. And the sons of Perez were: of Hezron, the family of the Hezronites; of Hamul, the family of the Hamulites.

22. These are the families of Judah according to those that were numbered of them, threescore and sixteen thousand and five hundred.

23. The sons of Issachar after their families: of Tola, the family of the Tolaites; of Puvah, the family of the Punites;

24. Of Jashub, the family of the Jashubites; of Shimron, the family of the Shimronites.

25. These are the families of Issachar according to those that were numbered of them, threescore and four thousand and three hundred.

26. The sons of Zebulun after their families: of Sered, the family of the Seredites; of Elon, the family of the Elonites; of Jahleel, the family of the Jahleelites.

27. These are the families of the Zebulunites according to those that were numbered of them, threescore thousand and five hundred.

28. The sons of Joseph after their families: Manasseh and Ephraim.

29. The sons of Manasseh: of Machir, the family of the Machirites-and Machir begot Gilead; of Gilead, the family of the Gileadites.

30. These are the sons of Gilead: of Iezer, the family of the Iezerites; of Helek, the family of the Helekites;

31. And of Asriel, the family of the Asrielites; and of Shechem, the family of the Shechemites;

32. And of Shemida, the family of the Shemidaites; and of Hepher, the family of the Hepherites.

33. And Zelophehad the son of Hepher had no sons, but daughters; and the names of the daughters of Zelophehad were Mahlah, and Noah, Hoglah, Milcah, and Tirzah.

34. These are the families of Manasseh; and they that were numbered of them were fifty and two thousand and seven hundred.

35. These are the sons of Ephraim after their families: of Shuthelah, the family of the Shuthelahites; of Becher, the family of the Becherites; of Tahan, the family of the Tahanites.

36. And these are the sons of Shuthelah: of Eran, the family of the Eranites.

37. These are the families of the sons of Ephraim according to those that were numbered of them, thirty and two thousand and five hundred. These are the sons of Joseph after their families.

38. The sons of Benjamin after their families: of Bela, the family of the Belaites; of Ashbel, the family of the Ashbelites; of Ahiram, the family of the Ahiramites;

39. of Shephupham, the family of the Shuphamites; of Hupham, the family of the Huphamites.

40. And the sons of Bela were Ard and Naaman; of

Ard, the family of the Ardites; of Naaman, the family of the Naamites.

41. These are the sons of Benjamin after their families; and they that were numbered of them were forty and five thousand and six hundred.

42. These are the sons of Dan after their families: of Shuham, the family of the Shuhamites. These are the families of Dan after their families.

43. All the families of the Shuhamites, according to those that were numbered of them, were threescore and four thousand and four hundred.

44. The sons of Asher after their families: of Imnah, the family of the Imnites; of Ishvi, the family of the Ishvites; of Beriah, the family of the Beriites.

45. Of the sons of Beriah: of Heber, the family of the Heberites; of Malchiel, the family of the Malchielites.

46. And the name of the daughter of Asher was Serah.

47. These are the families of the sons of Asher according to those that were numbered of them, fifty and three thousand and four hundred.

48. The sons of Naphtali after their families: of Jahzeel, the family of the Jahzeelites; of Guni, the family of the Gunites;

49. Of Jezer, the family of the Jezerites; of Shillem, the family of the Shillemites.

50. These are the families of Naphtali according to their families; and they that were numbered of them were forty and five thousand and four hundred.

51. These are they that were numbered of the children

of Israel, six hundred thousand and a thousand and seven hundred and thirty.

52. And the LORD spoke unto Moses, saying:

53. Unto these the land shall be divided for an inheritance according to the number of names.

54. To the more thou shalt give the more inheritance, and to the fewer thou shalt give the less inheritance; to each one according to those that were numbered of it shall its inheritance be given.

55. Notwithstanding the land shall be divided by lot; according to the names of the tribes of their fathers they shall inherit.

56. According to the lot shall their inheritance be divided between the more and the fewer.

57. And these are they that were numbered of the Levites after their families: of Gershon, the family of the Gershonites; of Kohath, the family of the Kohathites; of Merari, the family of the Merarites.

58. These are the families of Levi: the family of the Libnites, the family of the Hebronites, the family of the Mahlites, the family of the Mushites, the family of the Korahites. And Kohath begot Amram.

59. And the name of Amram's wife was Jochebed, the daughter of Levi, who was born to Levi in Egypt; and she bore unto Amram Aaron and Moses, and Miriam their sister.

60. And unto Aaron were born Nadab and Abihu, Eleazar and Ithamar.

61. And Nadab and Abihu died, when they offered

strange fire before the LORD.

62. And they that were numbered of them were twenty and three thousand, every male from a month old and upward; for they were not numbered among the children of Israel, because there was no inheritance given them among the children of Israel.

63. These are they that were numbered by Moses and Eleazar the priest, who numbered the children of Israel in the plains of Moab by the Jordan at Jericho.

64. But among these there was not a man of them that were numbered by Moses and Aaron the priest, who numbered the children of Israel in the wilderness of Sinai.

65. For the LORD had said of them: They shall surely die in the wilderness. And there was not left a man of them, save Caleb the son of Jephunneh, and Joshua the son of Nun.

Chapter 27

1. Then drew near the daughters of Zelophehad, the son of Hepher, the son of Gilead, the son of Machir, the son of Manasseh, of the families of Manasseh the son of Joseph; and these are the names of his daughters: Mahlah, Noah, and Hoglah, and Milcah, and Tirzah.

2. And they stood before Moses, and before Eleazar the priest, and before the princes and all the congregation, at the door of the tent of meeting, saying:

3. Our father died in the wilderness, and he was not among the company of them that gathered themselves together against the LORD in the company of Korah, but he died in his own sin; and he had no sons.

4. Why should the name of our father be done away from among his family, because he had no son? Give unto us a possession among the brethren of our father.

5. And Moses brought their cause before the LORD.

6. And the LORD spoke unto Moses, saying:

7. The daughters of Zelophehad speak right: thou shalt surely give them a possession of an inheritance among their father's brethren; and thou shalt cause the inheritance of their father to pass unto them.

8. And thou shalt speak unto the children of Israel, saying: If a man die, and have no son, then ye shall cause his inheritance to pass unto his daughter.

9. And if he have no daughter, then ye shall give his inheritance unto his brethren.

10. And if he have no brethren, then ye shall give his inheritance unto his father's brethren.

11. And if his father have no brethren, then ye shall give his inheritance unto his kinsman that is next to him of his family, and he shall possess it. And it shall be unto the children of Israel a statute of judgment, as the LORD commanded Moses.

12. And the LORD said unto Moses: Get thee up into this mountain of Abarim, and behold the land which I have given unto the children of Israel.

13. And when thou hast seen it, thou also shalt be

gathered unto thy people, as Aaron thy brother was gathered;

14. Because ye rebelled against My commandment in the wilderness of Zin, in the strife of the congregation, to sanctify Me at the waters before their eyes. These are the waters of Meribath-kadesh in the wilderness of Zin.

15. And Moses spoke unto the LORD, saying:

16. Let the LORD, the God of the spirits of all flesh, set a man over the congregation,

17. Who may go out before them, and who may come in before them, and who may lead them out, and who may bring them in; that the congregation of the LORD be not as sheep which have no shepherd.

18. And the LORD said unto Moses: Take thee Joshua the son of Nun, a man in whom is spirit, and lay thy hand upon him;

19. And set him before Eleazar the priest, and before all the congregation; and give him a charge in their sight.

20. And thou shalt put of thy honour upon him, that all the congregation of the children of Israel may hearken.

21. And he shall stand before Eleazar the priest, who shall inquire for him by the judgment of the Urim before the LORD; at his word shall they go out, and at his word they shall come in, both he, and all the children of Israel with him, even all the congregation.

22. And Moses did as the LORD commanded him;

and he took Joshua, and set him before Eleazar the priest, and before all the congregation.

23. And he laid his hands upon him, and gave him a charge, as the LORD spoke by the hand of Moses.

Chapter 28

1. And the LORD spoke unto Moses, saying:

2. Command the children of Israel, and say unto them: My food which is presented unto Me for offerings made by fire, of a sweet savour unto Me, shall ye observe to offer unto Me in its due season.

3. And thou shalt say unto them: This is the offering made by fire which ye shall bring unto the LORD: he-lambs of the first year without blemish, two day by day, for a continual burnt-offering.

4. The one lamb shalt thou offer in the morning, and the other lamb shalt thou offer at dusk;

5. And the tenth part of an ephah of fine flour for a meal-offering, mingled with the fourth part of a Hin of beaten oil.

6. It is a continual burnt-offering, which was offered in mount Sinai, for a sweet savour, an offering made by fire unto the LORD.

7. And the drink-offering thereof shall be the fourth part of a Hin for the one lamb; in the holy place shalt thou pour out a drink-offering of strong drink unto the LORD.

8. And the other lamb shalt thou present at dusk; as the meal-offering of the morning, and as the drink-offering thereof, thou shalt present it, an offering made by fire, of a sweet savour unto the LORD.

9. And on the sabbath day two he-lambs of the first year without blemish, and two tenth parts of an ephah of fine flour for a meal-offering, mingled with oil, and the drink-offering thereof.

10. This is the burnt-offering of every sabbath, beside the continual burnt-offering, and the drink-offering thereof.

11. And in your new moons ye shall present a burnt-offering unto the LORD: two young bullocks, and one ram, seven he-lambs of the first year without blemish;

12. And three tenth parts of an ephah of fine flour for a meal-offering, mingled with oil, for each bullock; and two tenth parts of fine flour for a meal-offering, mingled with oil, for the one ram;

13. And a several tenth part of fine flour mingled with oil for a meal-offering unto every lamb; for a burnt-offering of a sweet savour, an offering made by fire unto the LORD.

14. And their drink-offerings shall be half a Hin of wine for a bullock, and the third part of a Hin for the ram, and the fourth part of a Hin for a lamb. This is the burnt-offering of every new moon throughout the months of the year.

15. And one he-goat for a sin-offering unto the LORD; it shall be offered beside the continual burnt-offering, and the drink-offering thereof.

16. And in the first month, on the fourteenth day of the month, is the LORD'S Passover.

17. And on the fifteenth day of this month shall be a feast; seven days shall unleavened bread be eaten.

18. In the first day shall be a holy convocation; ye shall do no manner of servile work;

19. But ye shall present an offering made by fire, a burnt-offering unto the LORD: two young bullocks, and one ram, and seven he-lambs of the first year; they shall be unto you without blemish;

20. And their meal-offering, fine flour mingled with oil; three tenth parts shall ye offer for a bullock, and two tenth parts for the ram;

21. A several tenth part shalt thou offer for every lamb of the seven lambs;

22. And one he-goat for a sin-offering, to make atonement for you.

23. Ye shall offer these beside the burnt-offering of the morning, which is for a continual burnt-offering.

24. After this manner ye shall offer daily, for seven days, the food of the offering made by fire, of a sweet savour unto the LORD; it shall be offered beside the continual burnt-offering, and the drink-offering thereof.

25. And on the seventh day ye shall have a holy convocation; ye shall do no manner of servile work.

26. Also, in the day of the first-fruits, when ye bring a new meal-offering unto the LORD in your feast of weeks, ye shall have a holy convocation: ye shall do no manner of servile work;

27. But ye shall present a burnt-offering for a sweet savour unto the LORD: two young bullocks, one ram, seven he-lambs of the first year;

28. And their meal-offering, fine flour mingled with oil, three tenth parts for each bullock, two tenth parts for the one ram,

29. A several tenth part for every lamb of the seven lambs;

30. One he-goat, to make atonement for you.

31. Beside the continual burnt-offering, and the meal-offering thereof, ye shall offer them-they shall be unto you without blemish-and their drink-offerings.

Chapter 29

1. And in the seventh month, on the first day of the month, ye shall have a holy convocation: ye shall do no manner of servile work; it is a day of blowing the horn unto you.

2. And ye shall prepare a burnt-offering for a sweet savour unto the LORD: one young bullock, one ram, seven he-lambs of the first year without blemish;

3. And their meal-offering, fine flour mingled with oil, three tenth parts for the bullock, two tenth part for the ram,

4. And one tenth part for every lamb of the seven lambs;

5. And one he-goat for a sin-offering, to make atonement for you;

6. Beside the burnt-offering of the new moon, and the meal-offering thereof, and the continual burnt-offering and the meal-offering thereof, and their drink-offerings, according unto their ordinance, for a sweet savour, an offering made by fire unto the LORD.

7. And on the tenth day of this seventh month ye shall have a holy convocation; and ye shall afflict your souls; ye shall do no manner of work;

8. But ye shall present a burnt-offering unto the LORD for a sweet savour: one young bullock, one ram, seven he-lambs of the first year; they shall be unto you without blemish;

9. And their meal-offering, fine flour mingled with oil, three tenth parts for the bullock, two tenth parts for the one ram,

10. A several tenth part for every lamb of the seven lambs;

11. One he-goat for a sin-offering; beside the sin-offering of atonement, and the continual burnt-offering, and the meal-offering thereof, and their drink-offerings.

12. And on the fifteenth day of the seventh month ye shall have a holy convocation: ye shall do no manner of servile work, and ye shall keep a feast unto the LORD seven days;

13. And ye shall present a burnt-offering, an offering made by fire, of a sweet savour unto the LORD: thirteen young bullocks, two rams, fourteen he-lambs of the first year; they shall be without blemish;

14. And their meal-offering, fine flour mingled with oil, three tenth parts for every bullock of the thirteen bullocks, two tenth parts for each ram of the two rams,

15. And a several tenth part for every lamb of the fourteen lambs;

16. And one he-goat for a sin-offering beside the continual burnt-offering, the meal-offering thereof, and the drink-offering thereof.

17. And on the second day ye shall present twelve young bullocks, two rams, fourteen he-lambs of the first year without blemish;

18. And their meal-offering and their drink-offerings for the bullocks, for the rams, and for the lambs, according to their number, after the ordinance;

19. And one he-goat for a sin-offering; beside the continual burnt-offering, and the meal-offering thereof, and their drink-offerings.

20. And on the third day eleven bullocks, two rams, fourteen he-lambs of the first year without blemish;

21. And their meal-offering and their drink-offerings for the bullocks, for the rams, and for the lambs, according to their number, after the ordinance;

22. And one he-goat for a sin-offering; beside the continual burnt-offering, and the meal-offering thereof, and the drink-offering thereof.

23. And on the fourth day ten bullocks, two rams, fourteen he-lambs of the first year without blemish;

24. Their meal-offering and their drink-offerings for the bullocks, for the rams, and for the lambs, according to their number, after the ordinance;

25. And one he-goat for a sin-offering; beside the continual burnt-offering, the meal-offering thereof, and the drink-offering thereof.

26. And on the fifth day nine bullocks, two rams, fourteen he-lambs of the first year without blemish;

27. And their meal-offering and their drink-offerings for the bullocks, for the rams, and for the lambs, according to their number, after the ordinance;

28. And one he-goat for a sin-offering; beside the continual burnt-offering, and the meal-offering thereof, and the drink-offering thereof.

29. And on the sixth day eight bullocks, two rams, fourteen he-lambs of the first year without blemish;

30. And their meal-offering and their drink-offerings for the bullocks, for the rams, and for the lambs, according to their number, after the ordinance;

31. And one he-goat for a sin-offering; beside the continual burnt-offering, the meal-offering thereof, and the drink-offerings thereof.

32. And on the seventh day seven bullocks, two rams, fourteen he-lambs of the first year without blemish;

33. And their meal-offering and their drink-offerings for the bullocks, for the rams, and for the lambs, according to their number, after the ordinance;

34. And one he-goat for a sin-offering; beside the continual burnt-offering, the meal-offering thereof, and the drink-offering thereof.

35. On the eighth day ye shall have a solemn assembly: ye shall do no manner of servile work;

36. But ye shall present a burnt-offering, an offering made by fire, of a sweet savour unto the LORD: one bullock, one ram, seven he-lambs of the first year without blemish;

37. Their meal-offering and their drink-offerings for the bullock, for the ram, and for the lambs, shall be according to their number, after the ordinance;

38. And one he-goat for a sin-offering; beside the continual burnt-offering, and the meal-offering thereof, and the drink-offering thereof.

39. These ye shall offer unto the LORD in your appointed seasons, beside your vows, and your freewill-offerings, whether they be your burnt-offerings, or your meal-offerings, or your drink-offerings, or your peace-offerings.

Chapter 30

1. And Moses told the children of Israel according to all that the LORD commanded Moses.

2. And Moses spoke unto the heads of the tribes of the children of Israel, saying: This is the thing which the LORD hath commanded.

Matot

3. When a man voweth a vow unto the LORD, or

sweareth an oath to bind his soul with a bond, he shall not break his word; he shall do according to all that proceedeth out of his mouth.

4. Also, when a woman voweth a vow unto the LORD, and bindeth herself by a bond, being in her father's house, in her youth,

5. And her father heareth her vow, or her bond wherewith she hath bound her soul, and her father holdeth his peace at her, then all her vows shall stand, and every bond wherewith she hath bound her soul shall stand.

6. But if her father disallow her in the day that he heareth, none of her vows, or of her bonds wherewith she hath bound her soul, shall stand; and the LORD will forgive her, because her father disallowed her.

7. And if she be married to a husband, while her vows are upon her, or the clear utterance of her lips, wherewith she hath bound her soul;

8. And her husband hear it, whatsoever day it be that he heareth it, and hold his peace at her; then her vows shall stand, and her bonds wherewith she hath bound her soul shall stand.

9. But if her husband disallow her in the day that he heareth it, then he shall make void her vow which is upon her, and the clear utterance of her lips, wherewith she hath bound her soul; and the LORD will forgive her.

10. But the vow of a widow, or of her that is divorced, even every thing wherewith she hath bound her soul, shall stand against her.

11. And if a woman vowed in her husband's house, or bound her soul by a bond with an oath,

12. And her husband heard it, and held his peace at her, and disallowed her not, then all her vows shall stand, and every bond wherewith she bound her soul shall stand.

13. But if her husband make them null and void in the day that he heareth them, then whatsoever proceeded out of her lips, whether it were her vows, or the bond of her soul, shall not stand: her husband hath made them void; and the LORD will forgive her.

14. Every vow, and every binding oath to afflict the soul, her husband may let it stand, or her husband may make it void.

15. But if her husband altogether hold his peace at her from day to day, then he causeth all her vows to stand, or all her bonds, which are upon her; he hath let them stand, because he held his peace at her in the day that he heard them.

16. But if he shall make them null and void after that he hath heard them, then he shall bear her iniquity. These are the statutes, which the LORD commanded **17.** Moses, between a man and his wife, between a father and his daughter, being in her youth, in her father's house.

Chapter 31

1. And the LORD spoke unto Moses, saying:

2. Avenge the children of Israel of the Midianites; afterward shalt thou be gathered unto thy people.

3. And Moses spoke unto the people, saying: Arm ye men from among you for the war, that they may go against Midian, to execute the LORD'S vengeance on Midian.

4. Of every tribe a thousand, throughout all the tribes of Israel, shall ye send to the war.

5. So, there were delivered, out of the thousands of Israel, a thousand of every tribe, twelve thousand armed for war.

6. And Moses sent them, a thousand of every tribe, to the war, them and Phinehas the son of Eleazar the priest, to the war, with the holy vessels and the trumpets for the alarm in his hand.

7. And they warred against Midian, as the LORD commanded Moses; and they slew every male.

8. And they slew the kings of Midian with the rest of their slain: Evi, and Rekem, and Zur, and Hur, and Reba, the five kings of Midian; Balaam also the son of Beor they slew with the sword.

9. And the children of Israel took captive the women of Midian and their little ones; and all their cattle, and all their flocks, and all their goods, they took for a prey.

10. And all their cities in the places wherein they dwelt, and all their encampments, they burnt with fire.

11. And they took all the spoil, and all the prey, both of man and of beast.

12. And they brought the captives, and the prey, and the spoil, unto Moses, and unto Eleazar the priest, and unto the congregation of the children of Israel, unto the camp, unto the plains of Moab, which are by the Jordan at Jericho.

13. And Moses, and Eleazar the priest, and all the princes of the congregation, went forth to meet them without the camp.

14. And Moses was wroth with the officers of the host, the captains of thousands and the captains of hundreds, who came from the service of the war.

15. And Moses said unto them: Have ye saved all the women alive?

16. Behold, these caused the children of Israel, through the counsel of Balaam, to revolt so as to break faith with the LORD in the matter of Peor, and so the plague was among the congregation of the LORD.

17. Now therefore kill every male among the little ones, and kill every woman that hath known man by lying with him.

18. But all the women children, that have not known man by lying with him, keep alive for yourselves.

19. And encamp ye without the camp seven days; whosoever hath killed any person, and whosoever hath touched any slain, purify yourselves on the third day and on the seventh day, ye and your captives.

20. And as to every garment, and all that is made of

skin, and all work of goats' hair, and all things made of wood, ye shall purify.

21. And Eleazar the priest said unto the men of war that went to the battle: This is the statute of the law which the LORD hath commanded Moses:

22. Howbeit the gold, and the silver, the brass, the iron, the tin, and the lead,

23. Every thing that may abide the fire, ye shall make to go through the fire, and it shall be clean; nevertheless, it shall be purified with the water of sprinkling; and all that abideth not the fire ye shall make to go through the water.

24. And ye shall wash your clothes on the seventh day, and ye shall be clean, and afterward ye may come into the camp.

25. And the LORD spoke unto Moses, saying:

26. Take the sum of the prey that was taken, both of man and of beast, thou, and Eleazar the priest, and the heads of the fathers' houses of the congregation;

27. And divide the prey into two parts: between the men skilled in war, that went out to battle, and all the congregation;

28. And levy a tribute unto the LORD of the men of war that went out to battle: one soul of five hundred, both of the persons, and of the beeves, and of the asses, and of the flocks;

29. Take it of their half, and give it unto Eleazar the priest, as a portion set apart for the LORD.

30. And of the children of Israel's half, thou shalt take one drawn out of every fifty, of the persons, of the beeves, of the asses, and of the flocks, even of all the cattle, and give them unto the Levites, that keep the charge of the tabernacle of the LORD.

31. And Moses and Eleazar the priest did as the LORD commanded Moses.

32. Now the prey, over and above the booty which the men of war took, was six hundred thousand and seventy thousand and five thousand sheep,

33. And threescore and twelve thousand beeves,

34. And threescore and one thousand asses,

35. And thirty and two thousand persons in all, of the women that had not known man by lying with him.

36. And the half, which was the portion of them that went out to war, was in number three hundred thousand and thirty thousand and seven thousand and five hundred sheep.

37. And the LORD'S tribute of the sheep was six hundred and threescore and fifteen.

38. And the beeves were thirty and six thousand, of which the LORD'S tribute was threescore and twelve.

39. And the asses were thirty thousand and five hundred, of which the LORD'S tribute was threescore and one.

40. And the persons were sixteen thousand, of whom the LORD'S tribute was thirty and two persons.

41. And Moses gave the tribute, which was set apart for the LORD, unto Eleazar the priest, as the LORD commanded Moses.

42. And of the children of Israel's half, which Moses divided off from the men that warred.

43. Now the congregation's half was three hundred thousand and thirty thousand and seven thousand and five hundred sheep,

44. And thirty and six thousand beeves,

45. And thirty thousand and five hundred asses,

46. And sixteen thousand persons.

47. Even of the children of Israel's half, Moses took one drawn out of every fifty, both of man and of beast, and gave them unto the Levites, that kept the charge of the tabernacle of the LORD; as the LORD commanded Moses.

48. And the officers that were over the thousands of the host, the captains of thousands, and the captains of hundreds, came near unto Moses;

49. And they said unto Moses: Thy servants have taken the sum of the men of war that are under our charge, and there lacketh not one man of us.

50. And we have brought the LORD'S offering, what every man hath gotten, of jewels of gold, armlets, and bracelets, signet-rings, ear-rings, and girdles, to make atonement for our souls before the LORD.

51. And Moses and Eleazar the priest took the gold of them, even all wrought jewels.

52. And all the gold of the gift that they set apart for the LORD, of the captains of thousands, and of the captains of hundreds, was sixteen thousand seven hundred and fifty shekels.

53. For the men of war had taken booty, every man for himself.

54. And Moses and Eleazar the priest took the gold of the captains of thousands and of hundreds, and brought it into the tent of meeting, for a memorial for the children of Israel before the LORD.

Chapter 32

1. Now the children of Reuben and the children of Gad had a very great multitude of cattle; and when they saw the land of Jazer, and the land of Gilead, that, behold, the place was a place for cattle,

2. The children of Gad and the children of Reuben came and spoke unto Moses, and to Eleazar the priest, and unto the princes of the congregation, saying:

3. Ataroth, and Dibon, and Jazer, and Nimrah, and Heshbon, and Elealeh, and Sebam, and Nebo, and Beon,

4. The land which the LORD smote before the congregation of Israel, is a land for cattle, and thy servants have cattle.

5. And they said: If we have found favour in thy sight, let this land be given unto thy servants for a possession; bring us not over the Jordan.

6. And Moses said unto the children of Gad and to the children of Reuben: Shall your brethren go to the war, and shall ye sit here?

7. And wherefore will ye turn away the heart of the

children of Israel from going over into the land which the LORD hath given them?

8. Thus did your fathers, when I sent them from Kadesh-barnea to see the land.

9. For when they went up unto the valley of Eshcol, and saw the land, they turned away the heart of the children of Israel, that they should not go into the land which the LORD had given them.

10. And the LORD'S anger was kindled in that day, and He swore, saying:

11. Surely none of the men that came up out of Egypt, from twenty years old and upward, shall see the land which I swore unto Abraham, unto Isaac, and unto Jacob; because they have not wholly followed Me;

12. Save Caleb the son of Jephunneh the Kenizzite, and Joshua the son of Nun; because they have wholly followed the LORD.

13. And the LORD'S anger was kindled against Israel, and He made them wander to and fro in the wilderness forty years, until all the generation, that had done evil in the sight of the LORD, was consumed.

14. And, behold, ye are risen up in your fathers' stead, a brood of sinful men, to augment yet the fierce anger of the LORD toward Israel.

15. For if ye turn away from after Him, He will yet again leave them in the wilderness; and so ye will destroy all this people.

16. And they came near unto him, and said: We will

build sheepfolds here for our cattle, and cities for our little ones;

17. But we ourselves will be ready armed to go before the children of Israel, until we have brought them unto their place; and our little ones shall dwell in the fortified cities because of the inhabitants of the land.

18. We will not return unto our houses, until the children of Israel have inherited every man his inheritance.

19. For we will not inherit with them on the other side of the Jordan, and forward, because our inheritance is fallen to us on this side of the Jordan eastward.

20. And Moses said unto them: If ye will do this thing: If ye will arm yourselves to go before the LORD to the war,

21. And every armed man of you will pass over the Jordan before the LORD, until He hath driven out His enemies from before Him,

22. And the land be subdued before the LORD, and ye return afterward; then ye shall be clear before the LORD, and before Israel, and this land shall be unto you for a possession before the LORD.

23. But if ye will not do so, behold, ye have sinned against the LORD; and know ye your sin which will find you.

24. Build you cities for your little ones, and folds for your sheep; and do that which hath proceeded out of your mouth.

25. And the children of Gad and the children of

Reuben spoke unto Moses, saying: Thy servants will do as my lord commandeth.

26. Our little ones, our wives, our flocks, and all our cattle, shall be there in the cities of Gilead;

27. but thy servants will pass over, every man that is armed for war, before the LORD to battle, as my lord saith.

28. So, Moses gave charge concerning them to Eleazar the priest, and to Joshua the son of Nun, and to the heads of the fathers' houses of the tribes of the children of Israel.

29. And Moses said unto them: If the children of Gad and the children of Reuben will pass with you over the Jordan, every man that is armed to battle, before the LORD, and the land shall be subdued before you, then ye shall give them the land of Gilead for a possession;

30. But if they will not pass over with you armed, they shall have possessions among you in the land of Canaan.

31. And the children of Gad and the children of Reuben answered, saying: As the LORD hath said unto thy servants, so will we do.

32. We will pass over armed before the LORD into the land of Canaan, and the possession of our inheritance shall remain with us beyond the Jordan.

33. And Moses gave unto them, even to the children of Gad, and to the children of Reuben, and unto the half-tribe of Manasseh the son of Joseph, the kingdom of Sihon king of the Amorites, and the kingdom of Og king of Bashan, the land, according to the cities thereof with their borders, even the cities of the land round about.

34. And the children of Gad built Dibon, and Ataroth, and Aroer;

35. And Atroth-shophan, and Jazer, and Jogbehah;

36. And Beth-nimrah, and Beth-haran; fortified cities, and folds for sheep.

37. And the children of Reuben built Heshbon, and Elealeh, and Kiriathaim;

38. And Nebo, and Baal-meon-their names being changed-and Sibmah; and gave their names unto the cities which they builded.

39. And the children of Machir the son of Manasseh went to Gilead, and took it, and dispossessed the Amorites that were therein.

40. And Moses gave Gilead unto Machir the son of Manasseh; and he dwelt therein.

41. And Jair the son of Manasseh went and took the villages thereof, and called them Havvoth-jair.

42. And Nobah went and took Kenath, and the villages thereof, and called it Nobah, after his own name.

Masei

Chapter 33

1. These are the stages of the children of Israel, by

which they went forth out of the land of Egypt by their hosts under the hand of Moses and Aaron.

2. And Moses wrote their goings forth, stage by stage, by the commandment of the LORD; and these are their stages at their goings forth.

3. And they journeyed from Rameses in the first month, on the fifteenth day of the first month; on the morrow after the Passover the children of Israel went out with a high hand in the sight of all the Egyptians,

4. While the Egyptians were burying them that the LORD had smitten among them, even all their first-born; upon their gods also, the LORD executed judgments.

5. And the children of Israel journeyed from Rameses, and pitched in Succoth.

6. And they journeyed from Succoth, and pitched in Etham, which is in the edge of the wilderness.

7. And they journeyed from Etham, and turned back unto Pihahiroth, which is before Baal-zephon; and they pitched before Migdol.

8. And they journeyed from Penehahiroth, and passed through the midst of the sea into the wilderness; and they went three days' journey in the wilderness of Etham, and pitched in Marah.

9. And they journeyed from Marah, and came unto Elim; and in Elim were twelve springs of water, and threescore and ten palm-trees; and they pitched there.

10. And they journeyed from Elim, and pitched by the Red Sea.

11. And they journeyed from the Red Sea, and pitched in the wilderness of Sin.

12. And they journeyed from the wilderness of Sin, and pitched in Dophkah.

13. And they journeyed from Dophkah, and pitched in Alush.

14. And they journeyed from Alush, and pitched in Rephidim, where was no water for the people to drink.

15. And they journeyed from Rephidim, and pitched in the wilderness of Sinai.

16. And they journeyed from the wilderness of Sinai, and pitched in Kibroth-hattaavah.

17. And they journeyed from Kibroth-hattaavah, and pitched in Hazeroth.

18. And they journeyed from Hazeroth, and pitched in Rithmah.

19. And they journeyed from Rithmah, and pitched in Rimmon-perez.

20. And they journeyed from Rimmon-perez, and pitched in Libnah.

21. And they journeyed from Libnah, and pitched in Rissah.

22. And they journeyed from Rissah, and pitched in Kehelah.

23. And they journeyed from Kehelah, and pitched in mount Shepher.

24. And they journeyed from mount Shepher, and pitched in Haradah.

25. And they journeyed from Haradah, and pitched in Makheloth.

26. And they journeyed from Makheloth, and pitched in Tahath.

27. And they journeyed from Tahath, and pitched in Terah.

28. And they journeyed from Terah, and pitched in Mithkah.

29. And they journeyed from Mithkah, and pitched in Hashmonah.

30. And they journeyed from Hashmonah, and pitched in Moseroth.

31. And they journeyed from Moseroth, and pitched in Bene-jaakan.

32. And they journeyed from Bene-jaakan, and pitched in Hor-haggidgad.

33. And they journeyed from Hor-haggidgad, and pitched in Jotbah.

34. And they journeyed from Jotbah, and pitched in Abronah.

35. And they journeyed from Abronah, and pitched in Ezion-geber.

36. And they journeyed from Ezion-geber, and pitched in the wilderness of Zin-the same is Kadesh.

37. And they journeyed from Kadesh, and pitched in mount Hor, in the edge of the land of Edom.

38. And Aaron the priest went up into mount Hor at the commandment of the LORD, and died there, in the fortieth year after the children of Israel were come out of the land of Egypt, in the fifth month, on the first day of the month.

39. And Aaron was a hundred and twenty and three years old when he died in mount Hor.

40. And the Canaanite, the king of Arad, who dwelt in the South in the land of Canaan, heard of the coming of the children of Israel.

41. And they journeyed from mount Hor, and pitched in Zalmonah.

42. And they journeyed from Zalmonah, and pitched in Punon.

43. And they journeyed from Punon, and pitched in Oboth.

44. And they journeyed from Oboth, and pitched in Ije-abarim, in the border of Moab.

45. And they journeyed from Ijim, and pitched in Dibon-gad.

46. And they journeyed from Dibon-gad, and pitched in Almon-diblathaim.

47. And they journeyed from Almon-diblathaim, and pitched in the mountains of Abarim, in front of Nebo.

48. And they journeyed from the mountains of Abarim, and pitched in the plains of Moab by the Jordan at Jericho.

49. And they pitched by the Jordan, from Beth-jeshimoth even unto Abel-shittim in the plains of Moab.

50. And the LORD spoke unto Moses in the plains of Moab by the Jordan at Jericho, saying:

51. Speak unto the children of Israel, and say unto them: When ye pass over the Jordan into the land of Canaan,

52. Then ye shall drive out all the inhabitants of the land from before you, and destroy all their figured stones, and destroy all their molten images, and demolish all their high places.

53. And ye shall drive out the inhabitants of the land, and dwell therein; for unto you have I given the land to possess it.

54. And ye shall inherit the land by lot according to your families-to the more ye shall give the more inheritance, and to the fewer thou shalt give the less inheritance; wheresoever the lot falleth to any man, that shall be his; according to the tribes of your fathers shall ye inherit.

55. But if ye will not drive out the inhabitants of the land from before you, then shall those that ye let remain of them be as thorns in your eyes, and as pricks in your sides, and they shall harass you in the land wherein ye dwell.

56. And it shall come to pass, that as I thought to do unto them, so will I do unto you.

Chapter 34

1. And the LORD spoke unto Moses, saying:

2. Command the children of Israel, and say unto them: When ye come into the land of Canaan, this shall be the land that shall fall unto you for an inheritance, even the land of Canaan according to the borders thereof.

3. Thus, your south side shall be from the wilderness of Zin close by the side of Edom, and your south border shall begin at the end of the Salt Sea eastward;

4. And your border shall turn about southward of the ascent of Akrabbim, and pass along to Zin; and the goings out thereof shall be southward of Kadesh-barnea; and it shall go forth to Hazar-addar, and pass along to Azmon;

5. And the border shall turn about from Azmon unto the Brook of Egypt, and the goings out thereof shall be at the Sea.

6. And for the western border, ye shall have the Great Sea for a border; this shall be your west border.

7. And this shall be your north border: from the Great Sea ye shall mark out your line unto mount Hor;

8. From mount Hor ye shall mark out a line unto the entrance to Hamath; and the goings out of the border shall be at Zedad;

9. And the border shall go forth to Ziphron, and the goings out thereof shall be at Hazar-enan; this shall be your north border.

10. And ye shall mark out your line for the east border from Hazar-enan to Shepham;

11. And the border shall go down from Shepham to Riblah, on the east side of Ain; and the border shall go down, and shall strike upon the slope of the sea of Chinnereth eastward;

12. And the border shall go down to the Jordan, and the goings out thereof shall be at the Salt Sea; this shall be your land according to the borders thereof round about.

13. And Moses commanded the children of Israel, saying: This is the land wherein ye shall receive inheritance by lot, which the LORD hath commanded to give unto the nine tribes, and to the half-tribe;

14. For the tribe of the children of Reuben according to their fathers' houses, and the tribe of the children of Gad according to their fathers' houses, have received, and the half-tribe of Manasseh have received, their inheritance;

15. The two tribes and the half-tribe have received their inheritance beyond the Jordan at Jericho eastward, toward the sun-rising.

16. And the LORD spoke unto Moses, saying:

17. These are the names of the men that shall take possession of the land for you: Eleazar the priest, and Joshua the son of Nun.

18. And ye shall take one prince of every tribe, to take possession of the land.

19. And these are the names of the men: of the tribe of Judah, Caleb the son of Jephunneh.

20. And of the tribe of the children of Simeon, Shemuel the son of Ammihud.

21. Of the tribe of Benjamin, Elidad the son of Chislon.

22. And of the tribe of the children of Dan a prince,

Bukki the son of Jogli.

23. Of the children of Joseph: of the tribe of the children of Manasseh a prince, Hanniel the son of Ephod;

24. And of the tribe of the children of Ephraim a prince, Kemuel the son of Shiphtan.

25. And of the tribe of the children of Zebulun a prince, Eli-zaphan the son of Parnach.

26. And of the tribe of the children of Issachar a prince, Paltiel the son of Azzan.

27. And of the tribe of the children of Asher a prince, Ahihud the son of Shelomi.

28. And of the tribe of the children of Naphtali a prince, Pedahel the son of Ammihud.

29. These are they whom the LORD commanded to divide the inheritance unto the children of Israel in the land of Canaan.

Chapter 35

1. And the LORD spoke unto Moses in the plains of Moab by the Jordan at Jericho, saying:

2. Command the children of Israel, that they give unto the Levites of the inheritance of their possession cities to dwell in; and open land round about the cities shall ye give unto the Levites.

3. And the cities shall they have to dwell in; and their open land shall be for their cattle, and for their substance, and for all their beasts.

4. And the open land about the cities, which ye shall

give unto the Levites, shall be from the wall of the city and outward a thousand cubits round about.

5. And ye shall measure without the city for the east side two thousand cubits, and for the south side two thousand cubits, and for the west side two thousand cubits, and for the north side two thousand cubits, the city being in the midst. This shall be to them the open land about the cities.

6. And the cities which ye shall give unto the Levites, they shall be the six cities of refuge, which ye shall give for the manslayer to flee thither; and beside them ye shall give forty and two cities.

7. All the cities which ye shall give to the Levites shall be forty and eight cities: them shall ye give with the open land about them.

8. And concerning the cities which ye shall give of the possession of the children of Israel, from the many ye shall take many, and from the few ye shall take few; each tribe according to its inheritance which it inheriteth shall give of its cities unto the Levites.

9. And the LORD spoke unto Moses, saying:

10. Speak unto the children of Israel, and say unto them: When ye pass over the Jordan into the land of Canaan,

11. Then ye shall appoint you cities to be cities of refuge for you, that the manslayer that killeth any person through error may flee thither.

12. And the cities shall be unto you for refuge from the avenger, that the manslayer die not, until he stand before the congregation for judgment.

13. And as to the cities which ye shall give, there shall be for you six cities of refuge.

14. Ye shall give three cities beyond the Jordan, and three cities shall ye give in the land of Canaan; they shall be cities of refuge.

15. For the children of Israel, and for the stranger and for the settler among them, shall these six cities be for refuge, that every one that killeth any person through error may flee thither.

16. But if he smote him with an instrument of iron, so that he died, he is a murderer; the murderer shall surely be put to death.

17. And if he smote him with a stone in the hand, whereby a man may die, and he died, he is a murderer; the murderer shall surely be put to death.

18. Or if he smote him with a weapon of wood in the hand, whereby a man may die, and he died, he is a murderer; the murderer shall surely be put to death.

19. The avenger of blood shall himself put the murderer to death; when he meeteth him, he shall put him to death.

20. And if he thrust him of hatred, or hurled at him any thing, lying in wait, so that he died;

21. Or in enmity smote him with his hand, that he died; he that smote him shall surely be put to death: he is a murderer; the avenger of blood shall put the murderer to death when he meeteth him.

22. But if he thrust him suddenly without enmity, or

hurled upon him any thing without lying in wait,

23. Or with any stone, whereby a man may die, seeing him not, and cast it upon him, so that he died, and he was not his enemy, neither sought his harm;

24. Then the congregation shall judge between the smiter and the avenger of blood according to these ordinances;

25. And the congregation shall deliver the manslayer out of the hand of the avenger of blood, and the congregation shall restore him to his city of refuge, whither he was fled; and he shall dwell therein until the death of the high priest, who was anointed with the holy oil.

26. But if the manslayer shall at any time go beyond the border of his city of refuge, whither he fleeth;

27. And the avenger of blood find him without the border of his city of refuge, and the avenger of blood slay the manslayer; there shall be no bloodguiltiness for him;

28. Because he must remain in his city of refuge until the death of the high priest; but after the death of the high priest the manslayer may return into the land of his possession.

29. And these things shall be for a statute of judgment unto you throughout your generations in all your dwellings.

30. Whoso killeth any person, the murderer shall be slain at the mouth of witnesses; but one witness shall not testify against any person that he die.

31. Moreover, ye shall take no ransom for the life of a murderer, that is guilty of death; but he shall surely be put to death.

32. And ye shall take no ransom for him that is fled to his city of refuge, that he should come again to dwell in the land, until the death of the priest.

33. So ye shall not pollute the land wherein ye are; for blood, it polluteth the land; and no expiation can be made for the land for the blood that is shed therein, but by the blood of him that shed it.

34. And thou shalt not defile the land which ye inhabit, in the midst of which I dwell; for I the LORD dwell in the midst of the children of Israel.

Chapter 36

1. And the heads of the fathers' houses of the family of the children of Gilead, the son of Machir, the son of Manasseh, of the families of the sons of Joseph, came near, and spoke before Moses, and before the princes, the heads of the fathers' houses of the children of Israel;

2. And they said: The LORD commanded my lord to give the land for inheritance by lot to the children of Israel; and my lord was commanded by the LORD to give the inheritance of Zelophehad our brother unto his daughters.

3. And if they be married to any of the sons of the other tribes of the children of Israel, then will their inheritance be taken away from the inheritance of our fathers, and will be added to the inheritance of the tribe whereunto they shall belong; so, will it be taken away from the lot of our inheritance.

4. And when the jubilee of the children of Israel shall be, then will their inheritance be added unto the inheritance of the tribe whereunto they shall belong; so, will their inheritance be taken away from the inheritance of the tribe of our fathers.

5. And Moses commanded the children of Israel according to the word of the LORD, saying: The tribe of the sons of Joseph speaketh right.

6. This is the thing which the LORD hath commanded concerning the daughters of Zelophehad, saying: Let them be married to whom they think best; only into the family of the tribe of their father shall they be married.

7. So shall no inheritance of the children of Israel remove from tribe to tribe; for the children of Israel shall cleave every one to the inheritance of the tribe of his fathers.

8. And every daughter, that possesseth an inheritance in any tribe of the children of Israel, shall be wife unto one of the family of the tribe of her father, that the children of Israel may possess every man the inheritance of his fathers.

9. So shall no inheritance remove from one tribe to another tribe; for the tribes of the children of Israel shall cleave each one to its own inheritance.

10. Even as the LORD commanded Moses, so did the

daughters of Zelophehad.

11. For Mahlah, Tirzah, and Hoglah, and Milcah, and Noah, the daughters of Zelophehad, were married unto their father's brothers' sons.

12. They were married into the families of the sons of Manasseh the son of Joseph, and their inheritance remained in the tribe of the family of their father.

13. These are the commandments and the ordinances, which the LORD commanded by the hand of Moses unto the children of Israel in the plains of Moab by the Jordan at Jericho.